OTHER BOOKS ON JEWISH THEMES BY CHAIM RAPHAEL

Memoirs of a Special Case
A Feast of History
The Walls of Jerusalem
A Coat of Many Colours
The Springs of Jewish Life
The Sephardi Story
Festival Days: A History of Jewish Celebrations

Minyan

TEN JEWISH LIVES IN TWENTY
CENTURIES OF HISTORY

ABOUT THE TITLE:

Minyan

MINYAN is a Hebrew word meaning "number," which came to be applied to the quorum of at least ten men whose gathering together for prayer enabled the full service to be read. ¶ It seems just, in an extension of this use, to regard the ten Jewish men and women discussed in this book as a new kind of MINYAN —a MINYAN for all seasons.

Minyan

TEN JEWISH LIVES IN TWENTY CENTURIES OF HISTORY

BY CHAIM RAPHAEL

I. KING DAVID

II. HILLEL

III. MAIMONIDES

IV. DONA GRACIA NASI

V. MENASSEH BEN ISRAEL

VI. GLUECKEL OF HAMELN

VII. THE VILNA GAON

VIII. SIR MOSES MONTEFIORE

IX. EMMA LAZARUS

X. CHAIM WEIZMANN

Joseph Simon   Pangloss Press

Published by Joseph Simon/*Pangloss Press*
P.O. Box 4071, Malibu, CA 90265-4162

Designed by Joseph Simon
Illustrations by Manuel Bennett

Library of Congress Cataloging-in-Publication Data

Raphael, Chaim.
    Minyan : ten Jewish lives in twenty centuries of history / by
Chaim Raphael.
      p.   cm.
    ISBN 0-934710-28-7 : $27.50
    1. Jews—Biography. 2. Rabbis—Biography. I. Title.
DS115.R37   1992
920'.0092924—dc20   92-14078
                                         CIP

And Abram said:
Oh let not the Lord be angry,
and I will speak but this once:
Peradventure ten shall be found there.
And the Lord said,
Because of ten I will not destroy.

GENESIS 18:32

MY AIM IN THIS BOOK is to try to distill some personal meaning from the fact that as Jews living in the 1990's, we have immense epochs of identifiable history behind us. I will be exploring some of my feelings about this vast legacy by picking out ten prominent Jews—men and women—of the past twenty centuries whose lives I can interpret, to some extent, as benchmarks of every Jew's experience. Each represents a different phase of Jewish history, and inevitably there will be long gaps of time in between; but taken together they should add up, however briefly, to a unified projection of the whole story. I am grateful to the B.B.C. for encouraging me to offer this approach in a series of radio talks in 1991, and for permitting my use of some of the material.

CHAIM RAPHAEL

CONTENTS

		PAGE
	FOREWORD	11
I.	KING DAVID (C. 1000–C. 960 BCE)	15
II.	HILLEL (1st Century BCE)	25
III.	MAIMONIDES (1135–1204)	35
IV.	DONA GRACIA NASI (C. 1510–1569)	49
V.	MENASSEH BEN ISRAEL (1604–1657)	59
VI.	GLUECKEL OF HAMELN (1646–1724)	69
VII.	THE VILNA GAON (1720–1797)	79
VIII.	SIR MOSES MONTEFIORE (1784–1895)	91
IX.	EMMA LAZARUS (1849–1887)	105
X.	CHAIM WEIZMANN (1874–1952)	117
	FOR FURTHER READING	127

ILLUSTRATIONS

	PAGE
KING DAVID: *Then came all the tribes of Israel*	16
KING DAVID: *Give ear to my prayer, O God*	23
HILLEL: *Asked to explain the Torah by a pagan*	26
HILLEL: *The laws that were to govern Jewish life*	33
MAIMONIDES: *The Jews who converted to Christianity*	36
MAIMONIDES: *There was broad acceptance*	44
MAIMONIDES: *In all of his work*	47
DONA GRACIA: *Widowed in 1536 at age 26*	50
DONA GRACIA: *Helps the fleeing Jews*	58
MENASSEH: *Negotiated in London for the return of the Jews*	60
MENASSEH: *A small boat containing 23 Jews*	68
GLUECKEL: *Dear children, I began writing this*	70
GLUECKEL: *Appearance of a Jew called Shabbetai Zevi*	77
VILNA GAON: *A Maggid visited him in his sleep*	80
VILNA GAON: *Where Hasidism led*	88
MONTEFIORE: *A 19th-century Palestine Jew*	92
MONTEFIORE: *A Jewish lady of Gibraltar*	98
MONTEFIORE: *Remembering his past*	103
LAZARUS: *Drawn into passionate involvement*	106
LAZARUS: *Give me your tired, your poor*	112
LAZARUS: *The Jews filled the sweatshops*	115
WEIZMANN: *It was in student years*	118
WEIZMANN: *There are six million Jews*	124

MANY PEOPLE see Jewish history as a story of endless persecution, culminating finally in the deliberate massacre of millions of Jews—men, women and children—under the leadership of Nazi barbarism. If a different picture is presented in this book, it in no way softens the absolute evil expressed in the unbearable tragedy of our own day. To look positively at the richness of Jewish history is not to balance barbarism with happier themes. The evil can never be balanced or explained. Instead, as in a personal tragedy, one experiences a kind of balm by discovering the marvel of life itself.

With Jewish history, there is enrichment in understanding how the expression of Jewish life in so many forms built up over the centuries a meaningful power to survive. In this book we shall look at ten individual Jews, men and women, who are stages in that story, each making a wholly individual contribution to the underlying story—the continuum—in which the miraculous power of survival has found expression.

This personal approach will leave the way open for broader themes, uncovering a richness that can be triumphantly satisfying to those with a taste for history. If the meaning of being a Jew establishes itself at a personal level as a single continuous story, the fuller picture emerges as a confluence of enormously varied approaches. The story is then seen with far greater depth; and it is surely not in the least surprising that over a stretch of two—or even three—thousand years, there has been room for all kinds of different enlightenment, sometimes expressing conflict, but just as often emerging as a richer unified expression.

There is a unique symbol of this in the texture of the ancient "Talmud," a vast compilation of legal and anecdotal reportage that is constructed around tremendous individual argument yet adds up in the end to a positive exposition of one underlying theme: the rich joy of interpreting the Bible, partly by textual study but drawing in also ancient folk traditions transmitted orally. As one swims in the vast "sea of the Talmud"—now available in magnificent translation and commentary—it is astonishing to find that this ancient heritage, first edited nearly two thousand years ago, can furnish the same kind of intellectual and literary pleasure that has distinguished it from the beginning.

Jumping from ancient times to the historical themes of our own day, one finds the same kind of different approaches, in which one is encouraged to enjoy the conflict as much as the unity. The differences of interpretation become apparent in the most factual handbooks of Jewish history. A powerful example of this lies in the work of Salo Baron, much the greatest of our modern historians. On the "factual" issue, it is notable that in his huge *Social and Religious History of the Jews*, now totalling some twenty-five dense volumes, the scholarly notes available on each paragraph are almost invariably longer than his basic text, reflecting not only his meticulous record of sources in a profusion of languages, but the arguments between scholars on each subject, on which Baron finally gives his verdict.

It will be of interest to quote one such example, since the issue it deals with is so central to Jewish history. In the course of his introductory volume, Baron says (p. 23) that it is a fallacy to look back at the powerlessness of the Jews in the past as the equivalent of Jewish "despondency and misery" throughout the history of the dispersion. Until the Holocaust, the historian cannot give the Jews "priority" in suffering. Certainly they suffered, but not uniquely. Was it not the lot of all men, "especially in the dark and cruel ages of scarcity and horror, to suffer indescribable agonies"?

Baron is in fact prepared to go beyond this:

> It is quite likely in fact that the mediaeval Jew, compared with his average Christian contemporary, was the less unhappy and destitute creature, not only in his own consciousness but even if measured by such objective criteria as standards of living, cultural amenities, and protection against individual starvation and disease.

It is with this broad picture in mind that one can enjoy the richness of Jewish history as demonstrated now in the pioneer work of modern historians, much of which is produced in the ambience of the universities of Israel. Many of their books, often available in English, consist of detailed examination for the first time of ancient archives—Jewish, Christian, and Moslem—which testify to the richness of communal life. The most unexpected, perhaps, are the books of S.D. Goitein, based on the discovery in this century of the huge Arabic-script resources of the Cairo *Genizah* (storeroom), bringing the Jewish mediaeval world to light in the most delightful social detail.

Yet traditional scholarship in all these fields is by no means the only revelation. One benefits equally today from writers who have brought a new kind of literary imagination to understanding the familiar texts of the Bible. From the middle of the last century, much of this has been stimulated by archaeological discoveries of the Near East, yielding a host of comparative studies in linguistic and mythical fields; but often there are revelations of a different order. On the Bible itself, a new approach has been fashioned in books by Robert Alter on the narrative and poetic skills displayed in the text of the Bible. In a similar approach there is the work of Erich Auerbach in showing how the Biblical style—"fraught with background"— offers a gallery of characters whose psychological contradictions and multiplicity set the scene for the great character studies of western literature.

On a different level again, one finds rewarding "conflicts" in what one might call the philosophic approaches to Jewish history. From the days of the first destruction of Jerusalem two thousand years ago, there is a variety of Jewish writings which aim at fashioning a coherent response. Sometimes the approach is in the poetry of sorrow, as in the *Lamentations* of Jeremiah, or in the tear-drenched verses written to record the massacres of the Crusades. As time went on, sadness was deliberately turned into protest, as in the poetry written by Bialik at the time of the shattering Kishinev pogrom of 1903. In responding in this way to the Holocaust, a common theme remains bewilderment, though many try to weld this to some kind of positive understanding that can lie within the Jewish faith.

Sometimes a direct contrast reflects the fact that no single understanding of Jewish history can be received universally. There is perhaps an apt illustration from England in the contrast between the work of two distinguished writers, Sir Isaiah Berlin and Professor George Steiner. For Isaiah Berlin, expounding the history of ideas from his base at Oxford, all history, including Jewish history, yields an acceptable meaning only in terms of pluralism. "Monism" is meaningless: instead, one opens one's mind, as a westerner, to every approach that is consonant with the common morality that is tangible in the western world. To George Steiner, expounding ideas from his base at Cambridge, the meaning of Jewish history lies in its formulation of the Absolute. The undying expression of anti-semitism is, in his view, the "protest" of the non-Jewish world at having been set impossibly high moral standards from the days of Moses. For Steiner, then, the meaning of Jewish history is meta-physical. For Berlin, metaphysical concepts, either in the Bible or Hegel, do not seem to him to advance understanding.

It seems engaging to polarize Jewish thought in this Oxford and Cambridge fashion as an accompaniment from the sidelines to a book on the personal side of Jewish history. One realises from the book, and arguments outside it, that the continuum stretches far and wide, though it always adds up to the concept of *klal Israel*, the community of the Jewish people.

I

KING DAVID

C. 1000–C. 960 BCE

Then came all the tribes of Israel unto Hebron, and spake . . .
"Thou shalt . . . be a captain over Israel."

IN CHOOSING ten individuals from the wide realm of Jewish history, it seemed desirable to precede the story with an account of King David, even though he goes back a thousand years before the twenty centuries. I could say that I had to begin with him because the Jews have recited his Psalms endlessly as anthems of Jewish faith; but while this is indeed central, it is only part of the story. What is more important is that the feeling of being a Jew is rooted in David, in that two special expressions of one's life as a Jew flow from him with great power. The first is that in terms of religious faith, the Psalms of David plumb depths of feeling that go beyond the beauty of their language. The second is that although Jewish history began with the patriarch Abraham, David was the first leader, hundreds of years later, to unite all the tribes of Israel under one rule, thus moulding forever our consciousness as a people. The seeds of our faith lie in these two separate aspects of David's life, and each comes to us, through him, with complete intimacy.

A stranger thou shalt not wrong, neither shalt thou oppress him; for ye were strangers in the land of Egypt.

Exodus

This intimacy lies partly, of course, in the way we grow up aware of the Psalms in every phase of our lives. They are part of every religious celebration in synagogue; but they are also familiar to us in the celebrations of our family life, where the regular recital of this or that Psalm has grown into an enduring way of warming oneself with the feeling of that moment. Take, for example, the 126th Psalm, which is always chanted before the Grace after Meals, with no particular relevance except that it is so happy:

> When the Lord turned again the captivity of Zion, we were like them that dream.
>
> Then was our mouth filled with laughter, and our tongue with singing: then said they among the heathen, "The Lord hath done great things for them."
>
> The Lord hath done great things for us; whereof we are glad.
>
> Turn again our captivity, O Lord, as the streams in the South.

They that sow in tears shall reap in joy.

He that goeth forth and weepeth, bearing precious seed, shall doubtless come again with rejoicing, bringing his sheaves with him.

Give ear to my prayer, O God; and hide not thyself from my supplication.

Psalm 55

Sometimes a particular Psalm found its way into a ritual simply because its opening words fitted the occasion; but even then it was the poetry of the Psalm itself which generated an unforgettable mood. One example is the 114th Psalm, which we recite as part of the "Seder," the universally-enjoyed family gathering on Passover Eve. The opening words—"When Israel went out of Egypt"—are certainly appropriate, but within a moment the realism of this opening is taken over by the free-wheeling nature poetry which makes this Psalm so memorable:

When Israel went out of Egypt, the house of Jacob from a people of strange language:

Judah was his sanctuary, and Israel his dominion.

The sea saw it and fled, Jordan was driven back.

The mountains skipped like rams, and the little hills like lambs.

What aileth thee, O thou sea, that thou fleddest? thou Jordan, that thou wast driven back? Ye mountains, that ye skipped like rams: and ye little hills, like lambs?

Tremble, thou earth, at the presence of the Lord, at the presence of the God of Jacob;

Which turned the rock into a standing water, the flint into a fountain of waters.

But the Psalms are more than just poetry in an abstract sense. Behind the words, wonderful enough in the English of the Authorised Version, and more magical still in the original Hebrew, the Psalmist is communicating religious truths in the most human of terms, a concept which appeals as directly now as it did when they were first sung nearly three thousand years ago. Listen to the words of the very first Psalm—for there, in its recognition of failure as well as virtue, we find the broadest convictions of Jewish faith:

> Blessed is the man that walketh not in the counsel of the ungodly, nor standeth in the way of sinners, nor sitteth in the seat of the scornful.

> But his delight is in the law of the Lord; and in His law doth he meditate day and night.

> And he shall be like a tree planted by the rivers of water, that bringeth forth his fruit in his season; his leaf also shall not wither; and whatsoever he doeth shall prosper. The ungodly are not so, but are like the chaff which the wind driveth away. Therefore the ungodly shall not stand in the judgement, nor sinners in the congregation of the righteous. For the Lord knoweth the way of the righteous, but the way of the ungodly shall perish.

Lord, how excellent is thy name in all the earth . . .

Psalm 8

There are many other elements which contribute to this intimacy with David the Psalmist. We are totally at home with the Bible story of the distraught Saul finding comfort only in David's playing of the harp. And it is David we think of, even in Psalms that are obviously later than his time, like the famous Psalm 137, which tells of the exiled Jews weeping by the waters of Babylon when they remembered Zion. Even the rabbis, who are often thought of as being overwhelmingly legalistic, had a poetic attitude to David. There is a conversation in the Talmud which mentions that David used to recite a certain prayer on the stroke of midnight. And how did David know the time? A harp, one rabbi said, was suspended over his bed, and as soon as midnight arrived, a north wind came and blew upon it, and it played by itself.

There is, of course, more written about David in the Bible than about any other King, and the stories themselves are perhaps even more personalised than those of any other character. We see the earthy side—and even the dark side—of David very clearly; and this offers us a basis for the evaluation of the moral teachings that we expect to find at the heart of Jewish faith.

David, for us, brings to triumph the first phase of Jewish existence, stretching over hundreds of years from the vision that came to the

Patriarch Abraham in Babylonia, onward through slavery in Egypt, the Revelation to Moses at Sinai, the conquest of the Holy Land, and finally, under David, the first unified rule of this land.

Throughout the story, we see how the original Covenant between God and Abraham grew into the faith that David was to express later in his Psalms. The crucial moment in the story is, of course, the Revelation at Sinai; and it is certainly relevant to the Jewish sense of continuity that the Psalm which expresses the light and dark sides of consciousness most perfectly, Psalm 90, bears as its title: "A prayer of Moses, the man of God."

It is under the leadership of Moses in the Wilderness, that we meet for the first time the doubts and uncertainties of human conduct that were to be one of the main themes of the Psalms. At many points in David's own life, we are aware that his story has its shadowy side. The rabbis often talked of this, even if their dominant view of him was as the leader whose kingship was God-inspired. Kingship was always central. David himself, when fleeing as an outlaw from the jealousy of Saul, had always respected a certain holiness attached to the role of a king; and the theme of majesty which Saul represents, achieved its full form later both in the House of David itself, and in the city he founded: Jerusalem.

In some ways, it was this act of founding Jerusalem which remains the abiding symbol of David's power in Jewish life. Though the story of the capture of the site is told in purely adventurous terms, there is behind it a dramatic religious motif, for on this hill which David selected, the Temple would one day be built. The city of David was to become a holy city, the resting-place of the Ark of God. The Ark of God expressed the memory of the wanderings in the Wilderness. It had been an era of rebellion and sin, redeemed only by the presence of the Ark. In the intervening centuries, when "every man did what was right in his own eyes," the sense of a unified people had been lost. Now it was to be put on a wholly new basis by David's election as King.

With the greatest significance, David's election, by all the tribes of Israel, was at the already holy place of Hebron. It was in a village, now identified as Hebron, that Abraham had bought a burial-place from a local farmer that would establish his family's presence there for all time. Now, in this same place and with ancestral memories vivid in their minds, the elders of Israel annoint David as king:

> Then came all the tribes of Israel to David unto Hebron, and spake, saying "Behold, we are thy bone and thy flesh. In the past, when Saul was King over us, thou wast he that leddest out and broughtest in Israel, and the Lord said to thee: Thou shalt feed my people Israel and thou shalt be a captain over Israel."

Open my heart to your law, and let my Soul pursue your Commandments.

Talmud prayer

Yet even with this presage of power to come, the Bible picture of David carries forward much of the religious uncertainty of earlier ages. He is shown to us as a fountain of inspiration, but also as a real human being. Here is no abstract saintly figure, but someone whose words and deeds remain totally credible and intimate at every stage of his life. When the sons of Jesse are paraded before Samuel for the choice of a leader, God says to Samuel, when it is David's turn: "Look not on his countenance or the height of his stature; for the Lord looketh on the heart." We are immediately won over by these first words about the brave and charming shepherd-boy, but equally captivated when be hecomes part of King Saul's entourage, and the story takes on a new type of drama. In a heart-warming way, we see the deepening of David's friendship with Jonathan; but against this, Saul's jealousy of David's successes reaches such heights that David is forced to run for his life. Once he is King, he is faced with a problem that could only surface to someone in power: how to maintain autocratic rule in a moral way. His most dramatic failing on this score comes, of course, when he is captivated by the beauty of Bathsheba, and has her husband sent into the front line of battle, where he is promptly killed. What is significant is that we are told the story—which might not have been an unusual one for the time—for its consequence in moral terms.

In the first phase of the story, David himself is quite cynical about it, telling his captain Joab that this is the way things are, "for the sword devoureth one, as well as another." But to the Bible-writer, a major lesson has to be learnt. David has to be shown, by a brave man named Nathan, an embryo-prophet, that power will corrupt

21

unless it is governed by an inflexible moral code. When Nathan bursts into the King's presence to issue his rebuke in the form of a parable, David is suddenly made aware of the evil he has done. He is contrite, but this is not enough. To later generations of Jews, his moral failure was the key to the disasters that were to afflict David's descendants, exactly as prophesied by the courageous Nathan. "Thus saith the Lord," Nathan had cried. David had been given everything, and yet had despised the commandment of God. "Behold I will raise up evil against thee out of thine own house."

Blessed is the man that walketh not in the counsel of the ungodly . . .

Psalm 1

The stakes are high in the Jewish concept of David. At one level, he is an abiding presence for the pride that he evokes, but he is also a reminder that religious faith is more than a simple formula to help the believer comfortably through the problems of daily living. In terms of David's own life, we see that faith carries with it always the concept of a test, with the individual challenged to contemplate realistically the failures of human life, and the inscrutibility of Providence. The Psalms are full of this, and it is a heritage that forbids complacency. Read in this way, they can be a mirror of the sad story of David in his old age; but even so, we never forget the picture of David when we first meet him, a shepherd-boy bursting with life, "ruddy," the Bible says, "and withal of a beautiful countenance."

Give ear to my prayer, O God; and hide not thyself from my supplication. [Psalm 55]

II

HILLEL

1st CENTURY BCE

Asked to explain the Torah by a pagan while standing on one foot, Hillel said: "Thou shalt love thy neighbor as thyself. That is the entire Torah. The rest is commentary."

SOMETIMES a hero is unforgetable in a people's memory because of dramatic actions which leave their mark on the future. King David was certainly one such hero. But there are men who are central to the feeling one has as a Jew without dramas of this kind. A gentle teacher called Hillel, who lived at the turn of the Common Era—a thousand years after King David—was one such man.

Hillel was accepted in his time, and for many centuries after, as a perfect embodiment of the internal side of Jewish life. Apart from his authority as a scholar, he is beloved by Jews in a personal way through a few sayings which make it clear that he must have been both wise and tolerant in a very distinctive way. But his role really lies in having been the leader of the fellowship of Bible-teachers called "rabbis" who, between them, gave their fellow-Jews a key for survival in a period which might have spelt doom and oblivion.

In Hillel's own lifetime, the great Temple at Jerusalem was still the physical focus of Jewish existence, expressing both political independence under Roman suzerainty, and the celebration of the ancient religion with sacrificial rituals. Within a few decades of his death, this was all overthrown. The Jews had launched an all-out war against Roman domination. When the Romans brought the rebellion against them to an end, in the year 70 of the first century, they destroyed both the city of Jerusalem and its Temple.

Until our times, it seemed to Jews that this was the greatest tragedy of their history. No-one could have foreseen that it would be overshadowed in the 20th century by an evil far greater in its range. Until then, the Roman event dwarfed everything, and was known quite simply as the *Churban*, "the Destruction."

At the time of the Destruction, Jews were already living in many countries outside their homeland; but now, the loss of Jerusalem led the survivors into a new kind of existence, as wanderers and settlers

Whatever is hateful unto thee, do it not unto thy fellow. This is the whole law; the rest is commentary.

HILLEL

everywhere. It might have been expected that in these circumstances the Jews would inevitably lose their cohesion, but in the event, the Jewish faith remained inviolate. It was through the rabbis, with Hillel preeminent, that this happened. Through the teachings of the rabbis, Jewish existence had been transformed before the Destruction by a long succession of teachers who established a code of living and faith strong enough to hold its own in all succeeding centuries.

In a place where there is no man, strive to be a man.

HILLEL

The word "rabbi" is simply a term of respect meaning "Master." The rabbis were masters of Bible-teaching, turning study of the Bible into an all-embracing and very distinctive pattern of life. The teachings which emerged were grounded in the worship of God; but they expressed also a meticulous pattern of law, and the pursuit of every form of social responsibility. For the ensuing two thousand years, Jews have lived according to these teachings, guided very strongly after Hillel's day by descendants and disciples who were accorded a similar kind of authority. If it was, in one sense, group leadership for survival, the symbolic link historically was Hillel. It was his tradition that kept the Jews alive.

There are two senses in which Hillel symbolised the sustaining force in Jewish life. The first and most obvious is that in the many arguments that arose between the rabbis, the decision in any dispute almost always went according to Hillel's view. The second factor, less obvious at first, is that Hillel came from an upbringing in Babylonia, to join the fellowship of rabbis in the land of Israel. Babylon had already played an outstanding role in preserving Jewish identity after the *first* destruction of Jewish statehood, by Nebuchadnezzar, in 586 BCE, when a substantial part of the Jewish people had been exiled there. Although the Persian King Cyrus had allowed exiles to return later to their homeland, many stayed in Babylon and built up Jewish teaching there, with rabbis going back and forth to Israel. Hillel was one who moved west to the homeland in the first century BCE, and was soon elected there as head of a leading academy.

When we try to enter the mind of a teacher like Hillel, we have to remember that within the study of the Law, he and his fellow-rabbis had a deeper concern: what was to be the ultimate fate of their people? There could be doom ahead or there could be hope. Both had been expressed by the Prophets. Which would be predominant?

The political history of the Jews had started with King David ten centuries earlier. In these centuries, the future had always been uncertain; but it is safe to say that for Hillel, living before the Destruction, the over-riding outlook had to be one of hope, despite the prophecies of doom with which he and his fellow-rabbis would have been so familiar. The Prophets had brought this home in no uncertain terms. They had shaken David's successors and the people they ruled with a vivid picture of the punishment that would fall on them unless they mended their ways. With a mind alert to every verse of the Bible, a rabbi like Hillel had always to consider the weight of denunciation before he could move into hope. For the sense of doom, he could recall many an eloquent passage by the Prophet Isaiah:

> Woe unto them that draw iniquity with words of vanity, and sin as it were with a cart-rope . . . Woe unto them that call evil good, and good evil: that put darkness for light, and light for darkness: that put bitter for sweet and sweet for bitter . . . Woe unto them that are wise in their own eyes and prudent in their own sight . . . which justify the wicked for reward, and take away the righteousness of the righteous from him . . . Therefore as the fire devoureth the stubble, and the flame consumeth the chaff, so their root shall be as rottenness, and their blossoms shall go up as dust: because they have cast out the word of the holy One of Israel . . .

By itself, this remorseless denunciation would have been crushing to survival unless the Prophets had not portrayed their vision of hope with the same eloquence. Isaiah himself expressed this hope in words that have become immortal: "The leopard shall lie down with the kid, the calf with the young lion together, and a little child shall lead them." With equal beauty, the hope that sustained the Jews after the *Roman* destruction lay at hand in the words of the Prophet Jeremiah, who had chronicled the anguish of the *first* Destruction, but had had faith that this was not the end:

He who does not increase his knowledge— decreases it.

HILLEL

The Lord hath appeared of old unto me saying, Yea, I have loved
thee with an everlasting love: therefore with loving-kindness have
I drawn thee . . . Again, I will build thee, O virgin of Israel: thou
shalt be adorned with thy tabrets, and shall go forth in the dances
of them that make merry . . . Thou shalt plant vines upon the
mountains of Samaria, and shall eat them as common things . . .
Behold I will bring them from the north country and gather
them from the coasts of the earth, and with them the blind and
the lame, the woman with the child and her that travaileth with
child together . . . Hear the word of the Lord, O ye nations, and
declare it in the tales afar off: He that scattered Israel will gather
him, and keep him as a shepherd doth his flock. . . .

Here, then, was a stark portrayal of the two outcomes for the Jews;
but the ethical background that Hillel and his fellow rabbis drew on
had been broadened by his time into wider issues than the stark alter-
natives of punishment and hope. Hellenistic-Greek influences had
surged forward in the whole of the Near East from the end of the
4th century BCE; and like all other residents of these lands, the Jews
of Israel had absorbed something of this background. Greek was
widely spoken, Greek personal names were often used: Greek legal
and administrative terms were drawn on. And even though Jewish
teachers were extremely careful to rule out Greek practises that
might look like a bridge to the pagan understructure of the Hellenist world, we see from books quoted in rabbinic argument that an
awareness of Greek ideas had seeped through, even in Israel itself.
The rabbis undoubtedly gave careful reading on the one hand to a
Bible book like *Ecclesiastes*, which argues in a non-Jewish way for
the vanity of human existence, and on the other to the elegant
moralities of the *Book of Ben Sira*, with its Stoic outlook. For that
matter, they were concerned also with the religious problems raised
in the *Book of Job*, in which man's reaction to an apparently unjust
God is portrayed in a spirit that parallels Aeschylus in *Prometheus
Unbound*.

Job is in this sense the book furthest from "normal" Bible teaching;
but this is just one more reminder that beyond the basic moralities
of Pentateuchal law, there is no single accepted source for the overall
religious outlook of the rabbis, thus obliging us to construct a picture from varied sources. Perhaps the liveliest contemporary picture

is the one presented by the Jewish historian Josephus, who lived in Rome in the first century, and felt driven to contradict slanders on the Jews published by an Egyptian antisemite.

Josephus met the hostility of this writer and perhaps others by pointing to the virtues of Jewish life: industriousness, sobriety, mutual trust, care of the needy, and strong family ties. He went on to sum up the Jewish faith in these terms:

Judge not thy neighbour until thou art come into his place.

HILLEL

> I would therefore boldly maintain that we have introduced to the rest of the world a very large number of very beautiful ideas. What greater beauty than inviolable piety? What higher justice than obedience to the law? What more beneficial than to be in harmony with one another, to be a prey neither to disunion in adversity, nor to arrogance and faction in prosperity; in war to despise death, in peace to devote oneself to crafts and agriculture; and to be convinced that everything in the whole universe is under the eye and direction of God?

The words of Josephus certainly catch the flavour of the *social* attitude of the rabbis, and they equally bring out their respect for the *practicalities* of the good life, in contrast to the esoteric and apocalyptic ideas that had taken hold of the Hellenist world, with links later to the Christian faith. As against messianic speculation, the rabbis felt that study, pursued in humanistic terms, and with a deep respect for the law, offered the true assurance for the future.

The laws that were to govern Jewish life could be read in literal terms in the Five Books of Moses; but the intepretation of these laws was based on a long oral tradition, which allowed a teacher like Hillel to pass on to his disciples, and to future generations, a way of life that was more than dry law. The Gospels, written after the death of Jesus, have given the impression that the rabbis of his day, "the Scribes and Pharisees," left little room for humane interpretation of the law. But a very different picture emerges when one gets to know the sayings and style of a rabbi like Hillel. Take, for example, the reply he gave to a pagan who asked him if he would teach him the whole of the Torah while he stood on one foot. For an answer, Hillel turned to the Golden Rule expressed centuries earlier in the Pentateuch, and said to the pagan: "Thou shalt love thy neighbour as thyself. That is the entire Torah. The rest is commentary."

There is the same pithy flavour in another of his famed remarks: "Do not judge your neighbour until you are in his place." And even more pointed, and certainly witty, is a saying of Hillel's which is now so well-known that it has been turned into a kind of folk-song: "If I am not for *myself*, who will be for me? But if I am *just* for myself, what am I? And if not *now*, when?"

There is other evidence, too, which opposes the idea of the rabbis being totally legalistic. A warmer picture is conveyed in accounts of the joyous social life of the pre-Destruction centuries centered on Jerusalem. There is a lively example in the law book, "the Mishnah," edited in the 2nd century by a descendant of Hillel, and central to Jewish study ever since. Though it is basically a detailed handbook to the laws, it also describes the happy spirit in which these laws were put into action. Here is how the *Mishnah* describes the preparations for bringing the First Ripe Fruits to the Temple at Jerusalem, a festival pilgrimage that Hillel would have seen:

> The men of the smaller towns belonging to a pilgrim group gathered in one of the towns and spent the night in the open place of the town and came not into the houses; and early in the morning a local official said: "Arise ye, and let us go up to Zion, unto the Lord our God." The flute was played before them as they drew nigh to Jerusalem. When they had drawn nigh to Jerusalem, they sent messengers before them and bedecked their First Fruits. The rulers and prefects and the treasurers of the Temple went forth to meet them. And all the craftsmen in Jerusalem used to rise up before them and greet them saying: "Brethren, men of such-and-such place, ye are welcome." The flute was played before them until they reached the Temple Mount. . . . When they reached the Temple Court, the Levites sang the 3rd Psalm: "I will exalt thee, O Lord, for Thou hast set me up and not made mine enemies to triumph over me."

There are many equally happy pictures of pilgrim joys. All the pilgrims found rooms, we are told; no-one was called on to pay rent, since Jerusalem was seen as belonging to the whole of the Jewish people. No-one was ever heard to say: I have been unable to find

The laws that were to govern Jewish life could be read in literal terms in the Five Books of Moses; but the interpretation of these laws . . . allowed a teacher like Hillel to pass on . . . to future generations, a way of life that was more than dry law.

a stove for cooking the Paschal lamb. With these and countless other tales transmitted in the writings of the rabbis, it is little wonder that the love of Zion remained undying through the Dispersion centuries.

Hillel is particularly important in this field because, although he lived while the Temple of Jerusalem was still in existence, he stands in Jewish tradition as the teacher who expressed supremely the Torah teachings that were maintained in the Diaspora *after* the Destruction. Jews are fond of the trenchant attitude conveyed in his oft-repeated saying: "In a place where there is no man, strive to be a man": and that was something he was ready to do himself, by bravely interpreting the law so that it never bore harshly on the individual. Survival for the Jew came to be built around the holiness of study; and it is here that Hillel's academy, and his dynasty of descendants, remain so important in Jewish history.

III

MAIMONIDES

1135–1204

The Jews who converted to Christianity but clung to the old faith secretly, came to be known contemptuously as *Marranos* (swine).

Every hero or heroine of the Jewish past evokes a different kind of response in the mind of a Jew of today. With King David, as we saw, there is an awareness of majesty; with Hillel there is a gentleness behind his distinction as a teacher. Nothing as summary as this fits our approach to the next great figure in our roll-call, the 12th century philosopher Maimonides, known popularly by this name from a Greek appendix *ides* (son of) to his Hebrew name: Moses son of Maimon.

One might begin at first with a recognition that Maimonides was the most broad-based intellectual genius that Jewish history has ever known; but true as this is, our full response has to centre on him in ways less easy to summarize. One approach is to say of him that he was a unique *pivot* of Jewish thought. In a way unique to himself, he absorbed everything that had been significant until his day, transformed its form and content with ideas from outside Jewish life that enriched and reinforced the old traditions, and with all this in his mind, projected a pattern of Jewish self-awareness that would be authoritative, and at the centre of meaningful argument, in every century that was to come.

Historical developments around him played a major role in this. Maimonides lived at a time in which Jewish experience—and the world itself—had been transformed over five centuries by the rise to power of the new religion of Islam, unleashing political and social forces that had come to full flower in his day. For centuries before him, most of the Jewish people lived under the rule of Islam, and had long been absorbing and contributing to cultural developments in language, philosophy and science that had surfaced in this background. But side-by-side with this powerful form of joint participation, there was a palpable countervailing force of distinctively *Jewish* cultural identity, stimulated by the developments in general culture, but lifting Jewish cultural expression in some fields to heights not known before. Without the existence of these two countervailing forces, the uniquely fruitful role of Maimonides would have been impossible. It was central to his thought that this double background had to find

The Soul, when accustomed to superfluous things, acquires a strong habit of desiring others . . .

MAIMONIDES

37

a viable Jewish basis; and this remained an abiding characteristic of Jewish existence in all the centuries to come.

Jewish history is illuminated through the life of Maimonides from another important angle, in which one sees through him how the unity and spread of Jewish experience can transcend the life of one individual. He himself had been born in Cordova (Spain) in 1135, with his father, Maimon, a scholar descended from a long line of rabbis. This linked Maimonides to the flowering of Jewish secular learning under the mostly favourable conditions prevalent in Spain for at least three centuries. But if Spain was the birthplace of Maimonides, it was always significant for him that the Jewish culture of Spain drew great strength from the adjacent communities of North Africa, who in turn were in close contact with the talmudic background of Babylonia. When the peaceful position in Spain was interrupted by the rise to power of a fanatical sect of Moslems, known as Almohades (Unitarians), who ordered that Jews were to convert to Islam or be executed, Maimonides' father was among many who accepted token conversion in Spain while actively seeking refuge elsewhere. For Maimonides, then very young, this safe haven, after five or six years of wandering, was first in Fez (Morocco), and later in Egypt. It was this accessibility of the Jewish world that later enabled the influence of his writings to reach Jews everywhere.

The pattern of forced but doubtful conversion was re-enacted in Spain some centuries later when Christian rulers came to power over most, and then all of the country. As with Maimonides, thousands of Jews facing persecutions accepted conversion as the only way for survival. A large part of the Christian *conversos* who clung to the old faith secretly, came to be known contemptuously as *Marranos* (swine). Some became sincere Christians, but most were unhappy and began to seek an escape to some other country where they could openly return to their faith. The parallel with the earlier experience of Maimonides raised deep questions for Jewish history. In early writings, Maimonides had explored the position of Jews facing this grim alternative, and tried to lift their spirits by showing that a secret faith need never be sterile. A Jew in this position, he wrote, had to be on the alert always to escape, and in the meantime strengthen his courage by studying his faith with great intensity. He himself had demonstrated this approach by launching into his two most powerful books of scholarship—his major Code of Rabbinic Law and his philosophic *Guide to the Perplexed*—in very uncertain and dangerous conditions in Spain and Fez, before finding an established position in Egypt. It was significant also for the whole of Jewry that Torah study, in his view, had to be the centre of life for "ordinary" people and not limited to professional rabbis. In his own case he was adamant in refusing to be paid as a rabbi, and maintained himself by his exhausting practice as a doctor, with skills that led to his appointment, in his fifties, as house physician to Saladin's vizier.

Everything is foreseen, yet freedom of choice is given . . .

MAIMONIDES

In all of his work, both as philosopher and a doctor, Maimonides drew heavily, like his Arab contemporaries, on writings rescued from Greek classical times, and most notably on Aristotle. For some centuries, the Jews had played an important part in making Greek classical writings available to the world at large, using their knowledge of languages to promote translations across the spectrum of Greek, Latin, Arabic and Hebrew. This "first renaissance" of classical learning had already led to immense progress in all the sciences as well as in philosophy. Jewish scholars preceding Maimonides (especially in Babylonia) had made distinctive contributions, which were now taken a leap forward through Maimonides.

It was always a central issue for him to harmonize the liberated expressions of general culture in philosophy and science with basic aspects of the Jewish religion. The inheritance of Torah study and ritual observance had to be untouchable, even if at another level one was driven to follow human reason wherever it led. To put it in other words, he was a supreme rationalist who wanted also to benefit from "truths" projected by Moses and the Prophets in the Bible, that drew their validity from a source *beyond* reason. He conveyed this attitude in his statement about Aristotle that "he reached the highest degree of intellectual perfection open to man, barring only the still higher degree of Prophetic inspiration."

This had remained, of course, a central issue of religious philosophy. Maimonides found different ways of dealing with the problem, resulting sometimes in an open conflict of view with the Aristotelian approach (as on Creation), and sometimes moving subtly around the dilemma within Jewish life itself to offer "explanations" that would allow a rationalist to be at ease with tradition.

A major instance of the reliance by Maimonides on Absolutes emerges in his firm defence of the Bible view on the creation of the universe. For Aristotle, the universe had to be seen in terms of eternal existence, a datum that presented mankind with a challenge to consider endlessly the material "laws" that governed this existence. For Maimonides, the universe was created by God at a moment in time. It was *creatio ex nihilo*, before which nothing existed, as described in the Bible book of *Genesis*.

In resolving apparent conflicts of reason and tradition within Jewish life itself. Maimonides presented views that offered a way out to skilled philosophers but left concepts untouched for the "ordinary" man in the street. Two examples may be quoted on this, one dealing with the concept of life after death, the other with the conviction of Jews that the Messiah will one day come to transform existence.

Tradition was clear in both cases. On the after-life, it had been firmly believed from the days of the Pharisees and the early rabbis that at some point and in some form there will be bodily resurrection for the dead who have "earned" it, with much argument on which Jews (and non-Jews) should receive this blessing. In the oldest prayers, still in daily use by traditional Jews, God is hailed as One "who brings the dead to life." There was similar broad acceptance in prayer and simple faith that the arrival of the Messiah would be part of this world-to-come, which would be an existence of total material, as well as spiritual, happiness. Far from questioning these beliefs, Maimonides included them in a simple language Credo of thirteen points which he set out in an early work and which has been recited since mediaeval times in synagogue in the form of a very popular hymn known by its first word *Yigdal*. But if tradition has remained effective in this form, it is also important in assessing Maimonides to see how he expounded these two ideas at a more sophisticated level.

On bodily resurrection, it is significant that there is no mention of this in his *Guide to the Perplexed*. While claiming in various writings that he did not deny the traditional belief—he had to be cautious to avoid any charge of heresy—he was careful to stress that the mystery of an after-life could not be defined while man's soul was "imprisoned" in earthly existence. In philosophic terms, he saw immortality as an expression of the intensified intellectual consciousness which governs the universe. In this approach, a form of immortality can be reached even in *earthly* existence, through intense concentration on the spiritual issues of life, a view which was an essential part, also, of his ideas about the glories of the Messianic Age.

Numerous evils to which persons are exposed are due to the defects existing in the persons themselves.

MAIMONIDES

On the Messiah, he was offended intellectually by any thought of a miraculous Being whose arrival would herald the establishment of prosperity forever. The aspirations of a messianic age referred, in his view, to a blissful state in which the good life could be lived intensively. Torah study was the good life; and as it grew into something like universal participation, it would generate "messianic" happiness. Politically, this had to mean for Jews that they would be living in their own land, no longer subject to domination by other nations. Their ruler, a leader who would emerge into this role, would be a human being of the stock of David, and descendants would rule in the same humanist spirit. Prosperity would be expressed in humanist terms; and it was in this spirit that one prayed for the arrival of the Messiah, rejecting any claims of divine selection by adventurers who appeared from time to time.

One reflection of the dominant role of Maimonides in Jewish experience is that even in his lifetime he was communicating his views on all these subjects to distant lands, expounding Jewish law and philosophy, but also helping to boost morale in simple human terms. We know of this today because of the survival of letters, carried to far-off places between Jews everywhere. They used an astonishing "postal" system which grew in the Arab world as an integral part of the Jewish role in trade and finance. Much of this has come to light in relatively recent years through the discovery in a synagogue cupboard in Old Cairo of the *genizah* (stored) documents, covering trade, legal affairs, and a huge range of personal records out of which the great scholar D. S. Goitein evoked in his books a vivid picture of the times of Maimonides. One remarkable feature of Jewish participation in these trading arrangements was that Jews developed a widespread system of locally-based representatives, offering travellers a common background of Jewish law and mutual confidence, and acting as "consuls" in dealing with local rulers, a system which stretched, as we now know, from Spain to Arabia and the Far East.

One striking example of Maimonides' use of this system lies in a very long letter which he wrote, probably in 1172, to the leader of the Jews of Yemen in South Arabia, dealing mainly with a refutation of the attacks on the Jewish religion being made in that country by the Arab rulers, who were putting immense pressure on the Jews to convert to Islam or face execution. The substance of the letter provides detailed answers to the fallacious claims by Christians and Arabs that the Jews had perverted the true teaching of their own holy book; but Maimonides also deals in the letter with the claim of a pseudo-Messiah in Yemen that the intense persecutions were evidence that ordinary life was ending, and that he was poised to take over as the Messiah. This would-be Messiah was "mad," Maimonides wrote, and had to be rejected. As for the upheavals, Maimonides asked that his letter be sent to every country to give them faith. This indeed was done, with immense success. It is notable that though the Yemen letter draws on all the authority which Maimonides now commanded, he identifies in simple language with all their troubles. "The news of compulsory apostasy," he says,

> . . . has astounded and confounded the whole of our community. Our hearts are ashamed, our minds are confused, and the power of the body wasted because of the dire misfortunes which have brought religious persecutions upon us from the two ends of the world . . .

> You write that the hearts of some people have turned away: that their beliefs are weakened . . . Please give attention and consideration to that which I am going to point out to you that they may be established in unceasing belief. May the Lord deliver us and you from religious doubt. . . .

There is the same personal touch in a long letter which he wrote

42

in the other direction to a famed Jewish scholar of Provence (France), Samuel ibn Tibbon, who had translated the *Guide to the Perplexed* from Arabic to Hebrew, and had submitted questions to Maimonides on how to interpret certain passages. Once again it is a letter written with engaging friendliness:

> When your letters in Hebrew and Arabic reached me, I learned from them your clearness of mind and elegance of composition . . . All your questions were just, and all your conjectures with respect to the omission of a word, or words, were correct . . . I discern from your remarks that you have thoroughly mastered the subject, and that its inner meaning has become clear to you. I shall explain to you in Hebrew how you shall manage with the entire translation. "Give instructions to a wise man, and he will be yet wiser; be wise my son, and my heart also will rejoice."

Let no one think that in the days of the Messiah any one of the laws of nature will be set aside . . .

MAIMONIDES

It was by a happy accident of history that this southern area of France nurtured Jewish scholars who were at home with Arabic as well as French and Latin, and with a talent for translation. In the 12th century this prosperous area of France, the home of many old Jewish communities, was incorporated for a time into Catalonia, across the Pyrenees, which broadened the cultural interests of the Jews of Provence through the intellectual stimulus of the Jews of Moslem Spain. This was carried further when some Spanish Jews of the 12th century sought refuge in Provence from Almohad persecution, carrying with them, inevitably, the culture they had enjoyed, and which was now fed into the background of the Jews of Provence.

The impetus given to local culture by the immigration of a large number of refugees fleeing from persecution in a country of more sophisticated culture has, in fact, been a characteristic of Jewish history. The expulsion of the Jews from Spain in 1492 would itself provide a memorable illustration of this, bringing major benefits to a country, in this case Turkey, which welcomed them. In our own day, the flight of Jews from Nazi Germany to countries of refuge, notably Britain and North America, became, in time, a similar illustration of great benefit arriving in the wake of tragedy.

The effervescence of Jewish life is always, then, a principle to be

There was similar broad acceptance in prayer and simple faith that the arrival of the Messiah would be part of the world-to-come.

borne in mind when thinking of Maimonides. Nor have these movements of culture always been predictable in their style and effects. In Provence, for example, there had been a marked inflow of Jews earlier, from Ashkenazi (German) countries in the north, many fleeing from the persecutions of the period of the Crusades, but very welcome for the great expertise in Talmud study for which Ashkenazi Jewry was famous. An incidental result, however, was that this generated an intensely inward-looking orthodox strand in Jewish life in Provence, side-by-side with the more outward-looking influences flowing from their mingling with Jews from Islamic countries.

As a result of this there were, among the Jews of Provence, some who argued that the rationalism of Maimonides was heretical in tone; and a small but powerful movement grew there to have his work banned. Provence also saw the development of kabbalistic mystical ideas which ran counter to the rationalism of Maimonides; and this was an element in what grew into a strongly anti-Maimonist controversy.

In the long view, of course, these diversions in no way harmed the recognition that Maimonides had made a wholly original contribution to the feeling that Jews have about their faith. For centuries, the tenacious hold that tradition exercised on Jews had lain in rules and rituals developed by the rabbis in the age of Hillel; what Maimonides did was to deal with them in forms useable by both elite scholars and the masses. For scholars, he had produced, early on, a detailed picture of the "rules" as set out in the authoritative *Mishnah* (law book) of the 2nd century, with commentaries to make their meaning absolutely clear. Many earlier scholars had offered interpretations of this kind; but for Maimonides his powerful mind demanded that heterogeneous rules had to be expressed as one coherent system. At the top intellectual level, this was done in his own digest of Jewish law and practice, and in a different approach in his philosophic *Guide to the Perplexed*. But he was also impelled into setting out for the first time the "Articles of Faith" which every Jew could draw on without the resources of philosophy. In the *Mishnah* itself there is one brief conversational passage in which a group of rabbis consider the basic qualifications for Jewish fulfillment, one

Day after day at the break of dawn the majestic King sits and blesses the Holy Beings . . . Blessed be the hour in which I created you.

Hakhalot hymn

45

of which is a belief in resurrection. It was in commenting on this passage that Maimonides set out thirteen clear principles of belief which seemed to him to flow from the entire rabbinic background. These thirteen principles had an abiding influence. One expression of its appeal was that the list was turned, some centuries later, into the popular *Yigdal* hymn. More formally, they emerged as a 13-point Credo for personal recital, each article beginning with the words *Ani Ma'amin*—"I believe with perfect faith. . . ."

This introduction of a Credo was a wholly new idea. It was drawn from his marvellous self-assurance at the intellectual level; but it reflected at the same time a feeling that faith must reach Jews at the popular level in words, as well as in observance. This happens in a major way through the Jewish recital of the simple words of the *Shema*, a sentence from Moses' farewell address to his people. At a different level, *Yigdal* and *Ani Ma'amin* have the same impact.

Even in this brief summary it is evident that Maimonides was, and remains, a giant in Jewish history. His special place was that he summed up in his life and work the whole outcome of the remarkable Arabic period of "Sephardi" (Spanish-Jewish) history. Even in his own lifetime, the Christian re-conquest of Spain from the north had already absorbed a large part of Spain, with the Moslem era increasingly pushed back towards the final enclave in the south. For the future, it would be the *Christian* context which had to be considered.

Maimonides stands, then, for what might be called Part One of the Sephardi story. Part Two had equal distinction, though in a different mode. As we shall see, it left its mark very distinctively in time on Jewish—and also on world—history.

46

In all of his work, both as philosopher and a doctor, Maimonides drew heavily, like his Arab contemporaries, on writings rescued from Greek classical times.

IV

DONA GRACIA NASI

1510–1569

Dona Gracia . . . widowed in 1536 at the age of 26 . . . managed,
after some travels as a titular Christian, to find her way to Antwerp,
which was dominant in trade and finance.

IT IS PARTICULARLY agreeable in the climate of today that it is through the life of a woman, Dona Gracia Nasi, that we can reach some overall understanding of one of the most remarkable periods of Jewish history, an era linked in a special way to the Christian phase of the Sephardi (Spanish-Jewish) story, comprising triumphs and tragedies of unimaginable variety.

The historian Cecil Roth described Dona Gracia as "perhaps the most noteworthy Jewess in all history." Even a brief outline of her life establishes that she earned this judgment for her leadership in helping to rescue a large part of the Jewish people from the enormous upheavals that followed the collapse of the "golden ages" of Spain and Portugal. At the centre, large-scale conversion to escape murderous attacks had left the New Christians (known as "Marranos") exposed to the tortures of the Inquisition. This was followed in 1492 by total expulsion of all unconverted Jews.

The setting of Dona Gracia's life is enough by itself to explain the centrality of her role in Jewish history. She was born around 1510 in Portugal to a distinguished Spanish-Jewish family who had been among the many thousands who fled to Portugal after Spain expelled all its Jews in 1492. Within five years of the arrival of the refugees in Portugal, the promise of a safe haven with a free life as Jews was overturned by an edict, taking force in 1497, which allowed only those Jews who converted to Christianity to stay in the country. Mass conversion of many thousands then led to an amorphous existence which offered a tenuous security, and even a chance for some of a decent livelihood, if they could steer a safe way against the constant dangers of the Inquisition. Freedom to live more securely meant finding an escape route to countries free wholly, or partially, from the attacks of the Inquisition. This included the Low Countries, parts of Italy, and above all Turkey. Many ultimately arrived there, though often by a circuitous route which took years to follow safely.

Dona Gracia's life expressed this pattern perfectly. Widowed in 1536 at the age of twenty-six, and in sole charge of her deceased husband's substantial business in loans and gems, she managed after some

Set me as a seal upon thine heart, as a seal upon thine arm, for love is as strong as death.

Song of Solomon

51

travels as a titular Christian to find her way to Antwerp, which was dominant at the time in trade and finance. From there she moved after a while to Venice, and then in 1550 to Ferrara (Italy), where, through business and personal connections, she was able to secure the diplomatic protection of Turkey, and was thus free to revert openly to Judaism. She finally reached Constantinople, with her family, in 1553, and there, for the remaining sixteen years of her life, lived in quasi-royal style, free above all to devote her great resources to the rescue of Marranos in many parts of Europe, especially in some Italian cities, aided to a great extent by the support of the Sultan of Turkey.

In some ways, this dramatic story of danger and rescue has many parallels elsewhere in Jewish history. What makes it distinctive with Dona Gracia is that the Jewish passion she drew on had behind it the unique heritage of Sephardi cultural history which was vivid for her through generations of her family's leadership in Spain, and which has remained a dominant element in Jewish consciousness ever since. In this sense she is a symbolic figure, leading us into an evaluation of the quite remarkable culture which had first developed in Spain in the early Islamic centuries, but had then found a more variegated content as the spread of Christian rule saw the emergence of what was, in some respects, a tripartite culture, a symbiosis of Muslims, Christians and Jews. As Américo Castro, the great Spanish historian puts it, Muslims, Christians and Jews fell into roles that were essential to each other, even though each remained completely distinctive religiously, and socially separate.

The long participation of Gracia's family in Jewish cultural leadership is indicated partly by their name "Nasi," meaning "prince" in Hebrew, and thought to be a version of this title of honour in the past. With many of these "princely" families in Sephardi history, a dominant pattern was financial expertise on a large scale in working for various rulers over tax-collecting and loans, and a role as doctor and political adviser (even military leader sometimes) to these rulers, which made them extremely useful as communal leaders and spokesmen. Familiar, too, was the Jewish scholarship of these financial leaders, and their sponsorship of study in all its forms. Historians have recorded that of Gracia's ancestors one of them, with the Spanish name of Isaac Benveniste, had been body-physician to the kings of Aragon in the 12th century. Two centuries later, his descendant had been counsellor to Alphonso XI of Castile, while in the following century another ancestor of Dona Gracia's had put the finances of Aragon in order, and had enjoyed the representative title of "Court Rabbi."

. . . who are the remnants of your flocks?

JUDAH HALEVI

Dona Gracia's family moved on from this early status in Sephardi life to a wider basis in European finance, especially after she directed the family business following the death of her husband. As titular Christians after their forced conversion in Portugal, the family, now known as "Mendes," was able to take advantage of the immensely profitable opportunities which had opened up for Portugal through the discovery by Portuguese explorers (aided it is said by Jewish enterprise) of the sea-route to India around the Cape of Good Hope. The huge trade that then developed covered imports from the East of spices, gems, and luxuries, reshipped by Portuguese merchants to northern Europe and the Mediterranean. It was, in fact, along these routes that Dona Gracia and others seeking escape were able in time to develop their road to religious freedom, moving some of their trade quietly, first to north-west Europe, and on from there, after a time, to the now burgeoning Jewish centres of the Turkish empire.

The freedom of Sephardi leaders to participate fully at many levels in the political and intellectual elements in the world around them was in marked contrast to the inward-looking life at this time of the "Ashkenazi" (German) Jews in the north. The Islamic phase of Sephardi life had been crucial to their wider role. For though it was in the *Christian* phase of Sephardi life that the tripartite cultural symbiosis came into full flower, the outward-looking base had been characteristic even in Moslem times, as we see looking back to the life of a famed Jewish poet and philosopher called Samuel ibn Nagrela, who lived in the 11th century.

Ibn Nagrela was outstanding politically as vizier to the ruler of Granada, and leader of Granada's army in a victorious war against Christian Seville. What is significant for the passionately Jewish element in his life is that when his victory had been won he celebrated it in a very long Hebrew poem that saw his triumph as a direct parallel to the victory of Moses in his war against the Amalekites:

She stood at the roadside to receive the groaning wayfarers . . . so tired and weary,

I thank You now with song as when the king entered the fortress in his folly.

And thought to save himself in his stronghold . . .

But with God's sword my troops were successful, while his followers were by the sword cut down . . .

The princes dressed in fine linen touched with red were made crimson by arrows, and the assembly of the proud was coloured with blood . . .

I drank the cup of salvation, even that of my triumph . . . I put my trust and hope in You, my soul knows well Your glory and grace. . . .

The brilliance and variety of Hebrew poetry in the Sephardi heritage was particularly notable in these Moslem centuries. In Ibn Nagrela's own day, a younger poet and philosopher called Solomon ibn Gabirol produced during his short life a vast range of religious poetry, still popular in the Sephardi liturgy, in which the Hebrew was moulded by Hispano-Arabic conventions. More remarkably, a major philosophic work of his in prose called "The Source of Life" was translated from Arabic into Latin, and ascribed for centuries by Christian scholars to an Arab author they called "Avicebron" (their version of Ibn Gabirol), a mistake only discovered in the 19th century.

It is relevant to note that this religious side of Sephardi poets in the Muslim period was offset by their great love of secular poetry, especially wine-songs and love-songs, so popular in Spain. Indeed to get the full flavour of Dona Gracia's Sephardi heritage, one has to look beyond theology to this secular world, where one discovers countless nature and love poems in glorious Hebrew. An outstanding example is the work of an 11th century poet called Moses ibn Ezra, whose style can be seen in this brief extract from a "Wine Song for Spring":

The cold season has slipped away like a shadow. The rains are already gone, its chariots and its horsemen.

Now the sun, in its ordained circuit, is at the sign of the Ram, like a king reclining on his couch. The hills have put on turbans of flowers, and the plain has robed itself in tunics of grass and herbs . . .

Give me the cup that will enthrone my joy and banish sorrow from my heart . . .

Bring all day long, until the day wanes and the sun coats its silver with gold, and all night long, until the night flees like a Moor, while the hand of dawn grips its heel.

. . . every knee would have faltered but for this great House . . .

Elegy, on DONA GRACIA'S Death

Even Judah Halevi (c. 1075–1147), the greatest of the Hebrew poets from this period, had a secular side to his writing, though he took his place in the Sephardi heritage more decisively for the poetry he wrote expressing his love of Zion. The truth is that even in the creative Moslem years there was always an underlying uncertainty in their reception, which led the Sephardi Jews to think of themselves as exiles, dreaming of a return to the ancestral land. Among Halevi's numerous poems on this theme, his "Ode to Zion" was recited endlessly:

O Zion: will you not ask how your captives are, the exiles who seek your welfare, who are the remnants of your flocks?

. . . I am like a jackal when I weep for your afflictions; but when I dream of your exiles' return, I am a lute for your songs.

If the flow of lyrical poetry became less marked as time moved on, wealth, scholarship and political leadership showed the same trends that had been evident among the early ancestors of Dona Gracia. In this roll-call of leadership, the names of many famous families become legendary in Sephardi history. One thinks, for example, of the Abulafia family, whose leading representative in the 13th century— the kabbalist Todros ben Joseph Abulafia—had been saluted in contemporary Hebrew literature as "the prince of the Spanish *galuth* (exile)," and had served Alfonso X of Castile as foreign secretary.

In the 14th century, the current head of the family, Samuel ben Meir Abulafia, sustained King Pedro the Cruel of Castile through endless struggles with the nobility, and is remembered, among other things, for the magnificent synagogue he built in Toledo and which, with its long Hebrew inscription, survived as a church.

Perhaps the most remarkable family, epitomising, like Dona Gracia, the origins and international range of the Sephardi diaspora, were the Abrabanels (or Abravanels), whose wealth, wanderings and scholarship symbolised the whole period, encompassing Portugal as well as Spain, and establishing a particularly distinctive life after settling down in Italy.

After acting as royal treasurers in the 14th century for Cordova and Seville, and then in the same role in Castile, their decision to move as Marranos to Portugal before 1492 led them into a vast expansion of influence in that country. Typically, one of their members, Don Isaac Abrabanel, used his entire fortune in the service of the King of Portugal, but was famed also for his exceptional work as a Talmud scholar and classical humanist. Having transferred his fortune to Castile and becoming adviser to Ferdinand and Isabella, he put up a huge loan, in concert with another financial leader, Abraham Seneor, in a vain effort to avert the 1492 expulsion decree. Escaping to Naples, he was a royal adviser there too, but was mainly occupied, as he had been for years, in writing a large-scale commentary on the Bible. Settling in Venice, he organised a commercial treaty between Venice and Portugal, and wrote more books on philosophy and messianism. In the next generation, his son Judah—known as Leone Ebreo—practiced as a doctor but was fully identified as a philosopher and poet with the Platonic Academy of Florence.

The Sephardi life in Italy in this period had produced a Jewish renaissance in line with the general cultural renaissance flowing from that country. An intriguing aspect of this for feminists of today is that one hears of a number of Jewish women there fully expert in Jewish as well as in general studies. In Ferrara, for example, where Dona Gracia was finally able to emerge openly as Jewish in 1550, the outstanding personality of the community was Dona Benvenida, a member of the Abrabanel family and a great patron of learning in all its forms. The Modena family living there included Pomona Modena, as well versed in the Talmud, we are told, "as any man." Even more famous as a scholar was her kinswoman Bathsheba Modena, known as an expert in the writings of Maimonides, and even proficient in the mysticism of the *Zohar*.

Dona Gracia herself left no mark as a scholar, but carried with her, because of her close alliance with the Sultan of Turkey, diplomatic confidence that could outshine even the mighty Abrabanels. A notable illustration of this was her attempt to force the authorities of Ancona to reinstate the freedom from the Inquisition that Jews resident there had been granted by Pope Julius III in 1541. On the basis of this papal guarantee, Jews settled there in large numbers. When his successor Pope Paul IV withdrew the guarantee, with Marrano Jews being then arrested and sent to the stake, Dona Gracia saw to it that the Sultan of Turkey wrote a stern letter to the Pope asserting that the Jews there were under his diplomatic protection. When this failed to produce results, Dona Gracia sent messages to leading Jewish traders all over the eastern world asking them to boycott all trade with Ancona. Not all Jews followed her demand, but at least time was gained to find alternative solutions to the problem.

I looked at her throat, and there I saw a necklace full of Gems . . .

TODROS ABULAFIA, Spain

This was merely one part of her efforts to find safe haven for Marrano Jews. Side-by-side with this, she was heavily engaged in building houses, synagogues and study centres in all the Ottoman lands. Her outstanding success in this was the establishment of a very large Jewish community in Salonika, which from then on hosted a prosperous and colourful Sephardi population until the Nazis sent thousands from there to the death camps.

It was in Salonika, naturally enough, that a distinguished poet composed an elegy on Dona Gracia's death, expressing some of the feelings which all shared on the magnitude of her rescue work:

> She stood at the roadside to receive the groaning wayfarers who returned to the service of their Creator so tired and weary, that every knee would have faltered but for this great House. . . .

57

For herself, Dona Gracia's final desire was to be buried in the Holy Land, at a site she had chosen in Tiberias on Lake Galilee. In trying to build up Israel she was ahead of her time; but as "La Senora," the rescuer of her people, she had already allied herself very positively with the eventual rebirth of the ancestral land.

The people that walked in darkness have seen a great light; they that dwell in the land of the shadow of death, upon them the light hath shined.

ISAIAH, chap. 9

Dona Gracia helps the fleeing Jews to find new homes in other lands.

V

MENASSEH BEN ISRAEL

1604–1657

Menasseh ben Israel negotiated in London for the return of the Jews to England.

Readers of this book will probably have noticed that the author seems particularly liable to choose for discussion a character whose life is significant as a meeting-point for a number of highly varied streams in Jewish history as a whole. No one exemplifies this more clearly than the scholar and political activist Menasseh ben Israel, who lived from 1604 to 1657, with Holland as his base.

Separate not thyself from the community . . .

Ethics of the Fathers

In summation, one could evaluate Menasseh ben Israel for his acknowledged mastery from early youth of the whole range of Jewish studies; but a distinctive element becomes apparent immediately when we learn that he was warmly respected by non-Jewish leaders (Rembrandt painted his portrait) and was fully at ease with the secular and scientific learning that was coming to the fore in the 17th century. Like Maimonides five centuries before him, his independence of mind kept him from accepting any formal position as a rabbi. It was with his books—the first of which he published at the age of seventeen—that he opened up for the world around him a rich view of Judaism that was unshakeable at the centre but expressed at the same time a move to harmonisation with powerful ideas current in the world outside; and although the power of his mind could never approach that of his great predecessor, his feeling for the unfolding—and the propulsion—of Jewish history gave his life a style of its own.

Menasseh lived at a turning-point in *general* history, with Holland, his land of settlement, enjoying its growth of power before giving way to the emergence of England in this role. Menasseh, as we shall see, did his best to link these movements of power to the benefit of the Jewish people. Behind this awareness of history lay the dramas of his own family, in which his father before him, with direct results for Menasseh, had lived out a sadly familiar version of the Marrano story: conversion, a secret Jewish existence and a trial by the Inquisition, which he was lucky to survive as a "penitent." It was after these experiences that rescue came in the form of an escape to the relative peace of the newly emerged Dutch Republic, which had finally won its independence—with something close to complete religious freedom for Jews—after centuries of Spanish rule.

Menasseh's father had lived in Portugal as a "New Christian" under the name of Gaspar Rodriguez Nunes, before escaping to Holland with his two sons. Menasseh, the younger son, had been baptised in Madeira under the name Manoel Dias Soeiro. His father, on arriving in Holland, had taken a thoroughly Hebrew name, Joseph ben Israel, as so many Jews were to do in a similar reversion to independent life after the establishment of the State of Israel in 1948. Like the Biblical Joseph, he now gave his two sons the names Ephraim and Menasseh, recalling Biblical names with warm echoes in Jewish tradition.

Menasseh at twelve was a prodigy of Jewish study, with his first book at seventeen turning outward into "scientific" presentation of the principles of Hebrew grammar. This grew, following the trends of his time, into an assortment of Jewish and general theological books published, with himself as printer, in Hebrew, Spanish, Portuguese and Latin, with one strand aimed at reconciling contradictions in Biblical passages, and were very popular in Christian circles.

This questioning mind, with its anticipation of trends in Biblical scholarship in the 19th century, brings into the historical picture a more radical stream of thought that had already begun to be visible, with powerful and disturbing effect, in the background of the Jewish community of Holland. Overlapping Menasseh's time, two sincere thinkers in particular were illustrating a rebelliousness that Jewish life would repeat later as "emancipation" became more pronounced, with results that became very clearly marked as time moved on.

The first of the two who had showed this trend at an early stage in Holland was Uriel Acosta (1590–1640), member of a former Marrano family, who was moved by the new concepts of "naturalism" to reject the "unscientific" doctrines propounded by Bible teachings and entrenched by rabbinic authority. Among other things, he felt unable to accept a belief in personal immortality, a form of which, as we saw earlier, had been accepted as basic even by the rationalist Maimonides. For expressing his dissent, he was excommunicated by the Amsterdam community in very painful ceremonies. This persuaded him into recanting, so that he could enjoy a normal life; but even after this, he continued to express heterodox ideas, and was excommunicated a second time. Again he recanted, but the strain to his mind was too great, and he committed suicide.

A deeper and more organised rebel thinker, who was an actual contemporary of Menasseh, was Benedict (Baruch) Spinoza (1632–1677). While Acosta's thinking had been an appeal to reason in simple terms, as in arguing that the Bible miracles, and even its account of Creation, ran counter to basic scientific principles, Spinoza drew on his knowledge of science and contemporary philosophy to construct a wholly original approach to the relationship of Man and Nature which offered a view of ethics that was independent of the commands of a God as transmitted to a primitive people by a charismatic leader called Moses. Whereas Maimonides (whom he studied) had aimed at the synthesis of Reason and Revelation, but with Revelation as the *sine qua non*, Spinoza saw existence in terms of natural law, without any need for supernatural authority. His form of pantheism, which had no place for a personal God, turned to all nature as a basis for an ethical and free life, with reason untrammelled, as the basis for man's well-being. To the Church as much as to the Jews, Spinoza was an atheist who had to be rejected, even though his deep thought earned him great respect from contemporary philosophers. Like Uriel Acosta, he was excommunicated by the Jewish Amsterdam community, with no regard for his concern to promote an ethical life.

One inevitably regards these displays of intolerance as saddening in human terms, but it is easy to understand the bitter feelings that had been provoked in the community against those who seemed to reject out of hand the simple faith that had sustained the Jews in times of danger, and could not now be put at risk. Having won freedom from their precarious position under the Inquisition in Spain and Portugal, they were anxious that the Protestant world should not regard any of their community as subversive of established religion. To most of the Jewish leaders, and in all likelihood to Menasseh himself, philosophic scruples were less important than Jewish survival. This meant helping those still in danger, and discovering new areas for

A man who desires to help others by counsel or deed, will refrain from dwelling on men's faults, and will speak but sparingly of human weaknesses.

SPINOZA

a free Jewish life, an active concern that Menasseh himself promoted, as we shall see.

Amsterdam was a pivot on this in many ways. Beyond the home that it now provided for ex-Marranos and other Jews, historical developments were afoot through Amsterdam which in due course were to generate the great Jewish community of America. If Fate, in terms of a protective Providence, was operating this way, one had to help by every possible means.

The link at the time between Amsterdam and the future America had grown out of the great material prosperity which had blossomed in Holland and had driven the country towards colonial expansion. The earlier domination by Portugal in this field was giving way to the growing maritime and trade ambitions of Holland in both the Far East and across the Atlantic to the West. The ex-Marranos, drawing on wealth and international trade experience, were playing a substantial role in this, with shiploads of immigrants to Amsterdam increasing rapidly from the 1550's on, establishing new industries and taking a large share in both the East and West India Companies who financed trade and conquests. While the Jewish role was always marginal to Holland's growing eminence, it was significant enough to help at a crucial point in the establishment of a Jewish presence in North America.

Marranos had participated for some time in the Dutch settlements in Central and South America, maintaining contact always with their kinsmen in Holland. Though the Inquisition was rampant in Spanish and Portuguese colonies, there was some safety in being at a distance, and a chance of religious freedom when Dutch conquests took effect in various colonies.

Brazil was a case in point, with small but flourishing Jewish communities beginning to rise under Dutch protection in the north-east of this vast and potentially rich Portuguese colony, and with Jews prominent particularly in sugar and timber. When the area of Pernambuco was conquered by the Dutch in 1630, the Jews had gravitated there, rejoicing in new freedom. Portuguese forces worked for its recapture, and when this was finally achieved in 1654, the Dutch residents, including the Jews, were given three months in which to leave. Most Jews went back to Amsterdam, others settled in Caribbean islands, while a small boat containing twenty-three Jews set out for North America, arriving in desperate condition in New Amsterdam (the predecessor of New York) in September 1654, after surviving perilous attacks by pirates.

They were not yet safe, however, since Peter Stuyvesant, Governor of New Amsterdam, wrote to the Dutch West India Company expressing strong opposition to the idea of letting them stay. Many prominent Jews in Amsterdam had shares in the Company, and exercised their influence to allow the Jews to remain. The Governor was so instructed, and within a short time, the Jewish community put down firm roots, with immigrants coming now from many sources. This position continued when New Amsterdam surrendered to British forces in 1664, and became New York.

This was by no means the only interesting historical influence from Amsterdam that took place in Menasseh's lifetime. In a very different setting, an extraordinary Conference was convened by Oliver Cromwell in London in September 1655 to consider the re-admission to England of Jews, after a legal exclusion that had lasted for 464 years. Menasseh himself became the central instigator of this, drawing on both his wide acceptance as a leading Jew, and a strong personal involvement with a messianic issue which became an important underlying factor. Beyond making it possible, if his plan succeeded, to find a new home in England for a free Jewish existence, Menasseh "proved" that to have Jews in England fulfilled a condition for the Messiah to arrive. This earned it the support of a number of eccentric sects, active at the time in English religious thought.

Small Jewish communities had existed in many English cities in early mediaeval times, with some Jews drawn on by the authorities— including the monarchy, the Church and the nobility—for the unpleasant and dangerous role of funneling taxes and other funds towards their own lavish expenditures. In 1190 the King, having extracted what money he could lay hands on, issued an edict expelling all the Jews on pain of death. Despite this law, some Jews con-

65

tinued to be found in England in various guises, in some cases as crypto-Christians linked to a Spanish or Portuguese status.

In the wake of the Reformation, a passionate new interest in the Jews had surfaced in England, stemming basically from new translations of the Bible (particularly the 1611 "King James" version) now available easily to Protestant Christians, in contrast to the position in Catholic countries. This close familiarity had led to the development among Christian Bible readers of a whole host of sectarian religious and political views, expounded by a multitude of preachers and writers who were trying to guide the Christian world into the expectation of a new messianic era. One form of this concern with the Jews was linked to the hope of their conversion, so that a new unity of Bible believers would stimulate the Second Coming. This process saw the growth of many sects—like the Sabbatarians—who allied themselves in some ways to Jewish practices. A new importance was given to the study of Hebrew, with scholars looking to "Adam's language"—the first language of mankind, as they saw it—as the basis for a universal language. A fascination with Hebrew studies included the Christian study of the mysticism of the Kabbalah, which gave special meaning to every individual Hebrew letter.

A man who desires to help others . . . will speak at large of man's virtue and power and the means of perfecting them . . .

For some years Menasseh, while ruling out conversion as a step in the process, had been in active contact from Amsterdam with English scholars in this field. By something like an historical accident, he suddenly became involved with a development that led him to put English readmission on a wholly new foundation.

The key lay in his being able, through the discovery of America by Columbus, to give a new kind of realism to ancient legends about "the Lost Ten Tribes." The Bible describes how the ten tribes, constituting the northern kingdom of Israel, were carried off into captivity by Assyrian invaders (721 BCE) and never heard of again. The belief arose that the Messiah would only arrive when the lost tribes were found and reunited with the rest of the Jewish people. Many travellers had brought back "reports," which spread as legends, of their presence in remote places; but now a Marrano Jew brought back from Ecuador a story of meeting a community of natives liv-

66

ing deep in a forest who asserted that they recited the *Shema* and were true believers in the Jewish faith.

Since Columbus, the world had speculated endlessly on where the American natives came from. To see them as including the Lost Ten Tribes was sensational. The Marrano traveller met Menasseh and gave him a detailed account, to which he testified on oath. Menasseh decided that the story was true, and saw a link to England which was messianic in its possibilities.

The prophet Daniel had intimated (12.7) that the final Redemption would begin only when the dispersal of the Jews was complete "from one end of the earth to the other." In mediaeval Hebrew, this phrase, "end of the earth" was used loosely for England (Angleterre). If this country, currently without Jews, would readmit them, the scene would be set for the Redemption. Menasseh wrote a little book which he called "The Hope of Israel," to set out this thesis. He dedicated it to the English Parliament, and it had a wide readership when translated into English. Part of its success was due to the work of a Christian scholar, John Dury, one of Menasseh's closest friends, in working up the enthusiasm that led Oliver Cromwell to call the Whitehall Conference. As one writer puts it:

> The force of pamphlets, petitions and public opinion had wrested the question of Jewish readmission from the hands of theologians, millenarians, and outlandish theorisers of all persuasions, and placed it before the Protectorate of Oliver Cromwell.

The outcome can be seen as ironic. Menasseh himself came to England and was warmly received; but after listening to the arguments, Cromwell was reluctant to take a decision, being aware, perhaps, of the opposition of many merchants and some theologians. Without fanfare, however, Jews already in England with shadowy legality were permitted to stay, and buy a burial ground. The numbers began to increase; and the absence of a legal ordinance cancelling the mediaeval ban was providential in 1660, when the monarchy was restored under Charles II. All Cromwellian Orders were cancelled; but as the Jews had not received an Order of protection, there was nothing to cancel. Instead, they were free to enjoy henceforward a new kind of undefined but effective freedom.

Menasseh died shortly after the Conference, greatly saddened at what he thought was its failure. With hindsight, it was, on the contrary, a success, allowing a peaceful inflow to enjoy equal rights over a wide field, until the Jewish presence was formalised in the 19th century. In all these respects, it was one more example of the dynamism of Jewish historical development as symbolised by the life of Menasseh ben Israel.

There are halls in the heavens above, that open but to the voice of song.

Zohar

A small boat containing 23 Jews set out for North America, arriving in desperate condition in New Amsterdam in September 1654.

VI

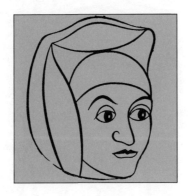

GLUECKEL OF HAMELN

1646–1724

"Dear children: I began writing this . . . after the death of your father."

IT IS PLEASING that in moving on in our story towards a new eminence in Jewish life of the Jews of northern Europe, a symbolic role can be given once again to a woman, a housewife and businesswoman known as Glueckel of Hameln. We know her through a delightful memoir she wrote about her life and times, which brings home to us the realities of Jewish existence in 17th century Germany, due to grow within two centuries into a momentous experience for the Jews of the world.

Glueckel's name indicates her husband's home in the small town of Hameln, not far from Hanover. She herself had been born in Hamburg in 1646 to a simple family with none of the inherited wealth and the long leadership traditions that had constituted the personal legacy of Dona Gracia. Nor was she able to become in any sense a figure on the international stage, able to play a major role in rescuing her people from the dangers of the Inquisition. Yet alongside this total contrast, there were underlying similarities between the two women both in character and as symbols of the built-in momentum within Jewish life.

With Dona Gracia, her final settlement in Turkey heralded the establishment in the Mediterranean world of a rich culture which drew on the distinctive roots developed in Spain, but went on from this to generate expressions of Jewish life in new forms as reflections of the vastly more varied backgrounds in which Sephardi Jews now found themselves. The parallel with Glueckel is that here too the Jewish spirit that surrounded her and was so clearly expressed in her own life was also poised for dramatic transformation. In Germany itself, the attachment of Jews to this land of long settlement and distinctive culture was already strong. This was due in time to bring both immense satisfaction and unspeakable tragedy. But with equal drama, Germany in Glueckel's day was rapidly becoming an immensely strong magnet of interest to the vastly proliferating centres of Jewish life in Eastern Europe that would lead in the future to both envy and disapproval. This broadening of the Jewish landscape, with Germany as a special focus, grew with increasing force after Glueckel's time.

These broad historical features are easily seen in hindsight. In Glue-ckel's own life, the dramas were mostly personal and small-scale. What makes her so significant for history is that obscure as she was herself, she left behind a book that brings to life the underlying structure of Jewish experience in her day. Her husband, who ran a flourishing business in gold and gem-stone jewelry, had died when Glueckel was forty-four. During the day she continued to take care of her eight children and also ran the business, which she knew intimately. In the evening she occupied her lonely existence by writing, in Yiddish, an immensely interesting memoir of her life and times, published for the first time two hundred years later, in 1896, and enabling us to see now the early strands in northern European Jewish life that were to be all-important as the centuries moved on.

I began writing this, with the help of heaven, after the death of your father . . .

Until the 17th century, the weight of Jewish life had lain in the Sephardi world. By the 18th century, and then with still greater power in the 19th century, this balance shifted overwhelmingly to the rapidly growing population of Eastern Europe, who developed in these centuries a civilisation that changed Jewish history. We read Glueckel's memoirs in the first instance for the delight they afford as a vivid picture of what was at the time a stable existence, though we also recall, through her book, the memory of past tragedies, absorbed by her time but certainly still lingering in Jewish memory.

Above all, her memoirs express clearly the foundations of Jewish faith that were taken by her as axiomatic and that were ultimately to prove, after enormous tragedy, the key to Jewish survival. In this sense, the roots of Glueckel's life had the same generative power as the traditions on which Dona Gracia had drawn. With both women, the pattern of faith developed by the rabbis many centuries earlier as a way of fulfilling the moral teachings of the Bible was still unshakeable. It was not long, as it happens, before a new approach began to develop in Germany among some Jews as a by-product of the European "Enlightenment" and its leaning toward "modernity." We are led on then, in thinking of Glueckel, to ask what were the elements that had kept the faith potent with particular power in Germany until her day.

One aspect of this was certainly the scattered nature of small Jewish communities spread over a very wide area in virtually total social and intellectual isolation from the general world around them. Though Jews had been resident in the Rhineland for many centuries as traders, and in a permitted—indeed required—role in financing loans, usually on a very small scale but sometimes with important institutions and individuals, it was always a tenuous existence linked to very fragile "rights" granted by those with local authority, including Church leaders, and liable to be completely disregarded at will. The same uncertainties governed Jewish life as Jews found similar trading and financial opportunities drawing them eastward into Central Europe.

But though this uncertain existence was a common pattern in many countries during the Middle Ages, some special factors in Germany had established an atmosphere of religious intensity not found at that time with the same force elsewhere. A major element in this was the incidence of the First Crusade that gathered force in the Rhineland in the early months of 1096 with murder and pillage of the Jews on a vast scale by Crusaders and camp followers inspired by the aspiration of rescuing Jerusalem from the rule of Islam. Jews, always thought of as killers of Christ, were readily available as targets of Crusader zeal, combining religious fervor with mob violence. A way of saving their lives by accepting conversion was almost always spurned by Jews under attack. One contemporary account of Jewish defiance in Mainz relates that "in a single day one thousand and one hundred Jews were slaughtered there." In addition to those killed by the mobs, a great number, seeing the fate that awaited them, committed mass suicide. In whatever form, they saw their death as a testimony of faith, for which the Hebrew expression is *Kiddush ha'shem* (sanctification of God). There was the same devotion on a massive scale as the Crusades moved on to other areas of Germany, to be echoed later in the Second and Third Crusades.

This was a searing experience for German Jews, leaving memories that never faded. One form of expressing their sorrow was the composition of many laments in elegiac Hebrew poetry recited to keep alive the sense of sanctification. One poem in memory of the martyrs of Mainz begins:

73

I shall speak out in the grief of my spirit before my congregation:
I shall wail and lament, for the Almighty has dealt bitterly with
me. Be silent, hear my words and my prayer. If only He would
hear me!

The Crusaders were massed at the gateway to blot out the name
of His remnants. Small children cried out to Him with one voice:
Hear O Israel, the Lord is our God, the Lord is One!

The poem, continuing for eleven eloquent and moving verses, is one
of many in the same tragic vein.

In more unusual form, the martyrs were remembered in the work
of a remarkable religious movement, unique in the Jewish world,
which bore the name of *Hasidei Ashkenaz*, "the pious ones of
Germany." It first took shape in the 12th and 13th centuries in
the Rhineland and quickly spread over most of Germany, and to
some extent to northern France also. Its literature took two forms,
one expressing intense devotion to the love of God by leading
an ethical life, while the second more distinctively explored esoteric
mysticism, secret doctrines as expressed later in *kabbalah*. With the
memory of the martyrs at the core, they hoped to lead their
followers towards the achievement of an unshakable state of grace,
with everything worldly giving way to an inner communica-
tion with God, expressed mystically in a drive towards self-abne-
gation. Some scholars believe that the forms of this intense devotion
indicate some contact with Christian religious thinkers, in ideas
developed by monks in contemporary brotherhoods and monasteries,
though no one knows how these contacts could have taken place.

A pious woman like Glueckel, living in the 17th century, undoubtedly drew on these deeply embedded German-Jewish roots, even
though as a bourgeois housewife and business-women she spent her
time, as her memoirs show, fully preoccupied with the worldly
affairs that the 12th century saints had turned away from. And indeed
Glueckel's real contribution to our feelings as Jews today lies, it
could be said, in demonstrating how unworldly extremism, as
evoked by an elite of teachers able to respond to life in this way,
gives way for "ordinary" Jews to a humane life-style that can be
both high-principled and yet tolerant and accommodating to others.

This more relaxed approach to the good life emerges on every page of Glueckel's memoirs. To get its flavour, we can pick out two episodes in this story, one related to a major Jewish issue, the other to an event in her personal life.

The public issue was the appearance in Turkey in 1665 of a Jew called Shabbetai Zevi, who claimed, or was willing to admit to ardent followers, that he was the Messiah. He had been trained in mystical lore, and exuded a great charisma in his preaching. The news that the Messiah had arrived spread everywhere, and persisted among many even after Shabbetai evaded execution by converting to Islam; but in the first news of his appearance, Jewish life had been dramatised by the feverish expectation that the Jews everywhere would be transferred magically to the ancestral land.

How great is a woman of valor; her worth is above rubies.

Proverbs, chap. 31

Glueckel, re-telling the story in her memoirs, exhibits a characteristic common-sense attitude, allied to a feeling of great sadness that such a marvellous event was not going to happen. The news had been brought to Hamburg and nearby towns like Hameln in letters sent from Turkey to Marrano refugees who had found their way to this area of Germany and established their own synagogues. "The joy when the letters arrived," she says, "is not to be described":

> Most of the letters were received by the Portuguese. They took them to their synagogues and read them out there. The Ashkenazi Jews, young and old, went into the Portuguese synagogues to hear them.

> The young Portuguese wore their best clothes, and each tied a broad green ribbon around his waist, for this was Shabbetai's colour. So all, with kettle-drums and round dance, went with joy to hear the letters read. Many people sold homes, hearth and everything they possessed awaiting redemption.

As an instance of the belief that the long journey to the land of Israel was now imminent, she describes how her father-in-law left his home in Hanover in the expectation of embarking from Hamburg:

> He sent us here two big barrels of linen ware, and in them were all kinds of food—peas, smoked meat, all sorts of dried fruits— that could keep without going bad.

These barrels were more than a year in my house. At last, fearing that the meat and other things would get spoilt, he wrote that we should open the barrels and take out all the food, so that the linen underneath would not spoil. . . .

But if she can smile a little in telling the story, she is extremely strict in defining the religious issue. The Messiah had not arrived, she says, because the Jews were too sinful to earn redemption. "Woe unto us for we have sinned. We did not live to see that for which we had heard and hoped to see." But the time will come, she says in a prayer to God: "Your people hope daily that You in Your infinite mercy will redeem us yet, and that the Messiah will come, if it be Your divine will to redeem Your people, Israel."

The more personal episode, in which her story brings her life to us as strongly as if the centuries did not exist, is her account of the wedding of her daughter, Zipporah, in Cleves, a town near Hamburg, to the son of an extremely prosperous Jew who lived there in a house "that was really like a king's palace."

It was a recurrent concern for Glueckel to marry off her daughters; and the negotiations on this marriage are described in fascinating detail. When the date finally arrived, the family set off fourteen days in advance, on a boat to Amsterdam for the first stage of the journey. We had "quite a handsome retinue" she says. There was Glueckel, with a babe at her breast; their rabbi, a man servant and a maid; and the ceremony, when it finally took place, was graced by high society. Prince Frederick, later to become King Frederick of Prussia, was staying with the Elector of Hanover, who had let it be known that they would like to be present. A frequently warm relationship with local rulers was one of the factors that contributed to the stability of life in that phase of German-Jewish history; and Glueckel's pride in this was a high point in her pleasure, especially since the Prince showed such admiration for her son Mordecai, then five years old. He was considered to be the most beautiful child in the world:

> The courtiers nearly swallowed him for admiration, especially the Prince, who held his hand for the whole time.

A public issue was the appearance in Turkey in 1665 of a Jew called Shabbetai Zevi, who claimed that he was the Messiah.

There was the same universal admiration for the bride, with Glueckel admitting that "she was really beautiful, and had no equal."

The wedding had taken place in the summer, close to the arrival of the Jewish Holy Days, starting with *Rosh Hashanah* (New Year); and this yields passages in her memoirs describing one of the most abiding absorptions in Jewish family life: the need to get home for *Yomtov* (the Festivals). The first problem in launching themselves on the long journey was to find accommodation for *Rosh Hashanah*, and *Yom Kippur* (Day of Atonement) a week later. With enormous difficulty, they finally found a place for *Rosh Hashanah*, but with no ship to get them to Hamburg by *Yom Kippur*. "The sea," they were told, "is full of pirate ships. They rob everything they can lay their hands on." At the last minute, Glueckel's husband secured a cart to take them to Hamburg by land; but with this problem solved, they had the same problem in getting to her father-in-law's house in Hanover, where they hoped to spend *Succoth* (the Feast of Tabernacles).

After various makeshift means of transport, a wagon was finally secured for the last eight miles to Hanover, and all their sufferings were over:

> My father-in-law came out to meet us. We saw him before we reached the town, like an angel, like the prophet Elijah, a staff in his hand, his snow-white beard reaching to his girdle, and glowing red cheeks. If one wanted to paint a handsome old man, one could not paint anyone handsomer. Our pleasure at the sight of him and our enjoyment of the festival are indescribable.

It is of great advantage that a person shall know his or her station . . . we seek relief from our own faults . . . we suffer from evils which we inflict on ourselves.

MAIMONIDES

VII

THE VILNA GAON

1720–1797

The Gaon once told a pupil that a *Maggid* had visited him in his sleep, and offered answers to a Talmudic problem he was studying.

I HAVE a strong personal motive in selecting the next figure in our *minyan*. Like so many millions of Jews in the world today, I trace my parents' roots back to the massive presence of "Ashkenazi" Jews in Eastern Europe in the 19th century.* The memory of the millions surviving to our time until slaughtered by the Nazis has made the attachment precious in a deeper sense. One knows it to have been a unique heartland of Jewish life, still vivid today in myriad forms for the heritage it communicated to the world. But how is one to break into this long story or choose an individual who can epitomize its evolution?

As a shepherd seeks out his sheep, so do you parade and count by number, and remember the life of every living thing...

New Year Prayer

There is one man, it seems to me, whose honorific title *"The Gaon of Vilna"* offers a possible step. The Hebrew word *Gaon* means "Excellency," and came to be used as a title marking great distinction. In this case it paid tribute to his phenomenal scholarship and saintliness of character; but there were also great historic reasons which we can draw on to illustrate his significance.

The Gaon's personal name was Rabbi Elijah ben Solomon Zalman, and his life spanned most of the 18th century, from 1720 to 1797. The keys to recruiting him for our *minyan* lie in the time and place of his life. The time factor is that he lived at a very significant point in the cycle of East European Jewish life. Over a period of more than 300 years, small settlements of Jews from a variety of sources had proliferated in Eastern Europe into a widespread but highly individual civilisation, sustained by its own language, Yiddish, adaptable to wholly new forms of life, and developing survival qualities that were to have immense potential for the future. In a fundamental sense, traditional rituals based on the Bible and rabbinic teaching were its lifeblood; and though the broad pattern of this life was found in many parts of Eastern Europe, it was from the Gaon's Vilna—"the Jerusalem of the north"—that this deeply embedded outlook had communicated its most intense expression.

*In mediaeval Hebrew, a Bible place-name "Ashkenaz" came to be used for Germany, and hence for Jews from Germany who moved eastward across Europe even without direct German connections. Jews from around the Mediterranean and to the East came to be known as "Sephardi," from Hebrew "Sepharad," used for Spain.

81

The Gaon's life can be seen, then, as drawing on a powerful background of the past; but it can also be seen as a significant staging-point in a number of ways for the era which followed. Until the 18th century, the Ashkenazi Jews of Eastern Europe had been largely inward-looking, in clear contrast to the Sephardi Jews of the south, a great many of whom had strong intellectual and even social involvements with the non-Jews among whom they lived. The isolation of the Gaon's world did not disappear in his time, yet was poised for change. It is certainly symbolic that the Gaon lived at the time of the French Revolution, due to prove immensely disturbing to political stability everywhere. More relevantly for the Gaon himself, it was a time in which a number of "outward-looking" German Jews had begun in a tentative way to adopt ideas stimulated by the European "Enlightenment," in a movement of their own called *Haskalah*. The Jews of Eastern Europe proved very slow to move in this direction. The Gaon himself rejected everything which might smack of *Haskalah*, and it was a long time before influences of this kind became fully active in Eastern Europe. Indeed, a new movement called "Hasidism" which spread in the Gaon's day in Eastern Europe was, as we shall see, the very opposite of *Haskalah*.

Yet the Gaon can still be seen as involved meaningfully in the liberation of Jewish thought from its exclusive inward-looking frame. To understand this paradox, we have to consider some special qualities of his teaching which were to be a harbinger of the future.

The issue turned for him, and continues to turn now, on the place of reason in the Jewish faith. It would miss the point completely to portray this as an argument between believers in God and rationalist sceptics. The Gaon was the most devout believer in God imaginable, but he was also strongly affected by what he saw as the God-given power of human reason. If this seems a paradox, it can perhaps be understood by noting his constant drive to unearth the inner meaning of the Bible. He wrote many commentaries on individual Bible books side-by-side with his endless rabbinic writings, all unpublished in his lifetime and preserved by devoted disciples. In his view, the Bible that has come down to us has to be accepted as the straight word of God in every jot and tittle; yet man is called on to explore ceaselessly, through the power of reason, every possible interpretation of its words. The interpretation has to include a deep respect for oral traditions, and their expression in law and rituals. In addition, the full use of of man's reasoning power means that one has to take note of how different scholars have expressed their views over the ages, and measure one's own views with this accumulated wisdom in mind.

An anecdote is told of the Gaon which perhaps illuminates this approach in an unexpected way. There had been a revival for some time of "kabbalistic" mystic ideas in the Jewish world, with messianic overtones that had led to the emergence in Turkey of a pseudo-messiah, Shabbetai Zevi, whose fame had erupted suddenly in the 1660's, a century before the Gaon. The Gaon was totally opposed, as we shall see, to what he saw as misuse of mystic ideas by the Hasidic folk-movement, which had spread rapidly in his day; but he had studied *kabbalah* in a scholarly way, and did not entirely reject claims of some learned kabbalists that they were visited in dreams by a heavenly mentor (a *maggid*) who gave them learned revelations which they subsequently drew on in their studies. The Gaon himself had once told a favourite pupil that a *maggid* had visited *him* in his sleep, and offered answers to a Talmud problem he was studying. He had declined the offer, he said. He wanted the answers to come to him by his own reason, and not on a plate.

The emphasis that the Vilna Gaon gave in this attitude to the pride that humanity should feel, and exercise, in having the universe opened up by innate human powers has reminded me from time to time of a sermon delivered a century earlier in London's St. Paul's Cathedral by the poet and cleric John Donne, in which he took issue rather belligerently with the famous verse in the 8th Psalm: "What is man that Thou art mindful of him?" Donne, as one would expect, is reverential in his own way:

> David asks the question with a holy wonder: *Quid est homo?* What is man that God is so mindful of him? But I may have his leave to say, since God is so mindful of him, since God hath set his mind upon him; What is *not* Man? Man is all.

Would the Vilna Gaon have agreed if he had heard this view? I think so, in the form in which Donne moved into the full force of his argument:

> For man is not only a contributory Creature but a total Creature.
> He is not a piece of the world, but the world itself; and next to
> the glory of God, the reason why there is a world.

This can perhaps be linked to the Gaon's legacy by mentioning a historical development that seems very much in tune with his approach. It is notable that within a few generations after the Gaon, descendants of his rabbinic background in Eastern Europe have included some of the most outstanding scholars and scientists of the modern world. To many, it seems that this is a product of the same process which absorbed Talmud scholars there day and night in the most refined intellectual argument. A pattern of deep study was being set, that would spread out into many different fields, once the isolation of Eastern European Jews was relaxed. The Gaon himself had rejected the mediaeval logic-chopping style of earlier talmudists, and relied on penetrating but straight-forward interpretation which might be aided, he thought, by insights into nature provided by science—chemistry, mathematics, astronomy and the like. The books on these subjects that he got hold of were inevitably out of date, but he was showing to the credulous and superstitious the path Jewish life should follow—a prophet indeed of what actually happened.

There is another major respect in which the life of the Jews of Eastern Europe had laid the base, far more than is usually imagined, for the move to a more open society. Most people have accepted an image of that world which concentrates on the isolation and poverty of the Jews living either in urban ghettoes or in remote *shtetls* (village townlets), and dominated in every respect by the built-in hostility of all who surrounded them—church authorities, the nobility, rival merchants, and perhaps above all, the peasants. No one would deny that this burning hostility was always a feature of life for the Jews, rising to peak oppression in some periods, as in the Chmielnicki massacres of 1648–49 in the Ukraine, and later in the mounting toll of officially inspired pogroms. But while this story of persecution is painfully true in all these respects, it is still far too bald a description of the Jewish experience of that world, in that it leaves out the dynamism which had prompted the spread of the Jews into both the central and remote reaches of these vast territories, and made the Jews an integral element in their economic development. It is a tragedy that the multi-varied role of the Jews in this field had a share in stimulating the underlying hatred which they experienced; but a wholly negative picture would leave unexplained the force that led them into an astonishing expansion of their populations, with resources and connections which they would draw on productively for many decades after the Gaon's time, until confronted with the overwhelming odds of pogroms and Nazi annihilations.

According to the Jewish view, what exists is in existence because of the will of the Creator.

MAIMONIDES

The favourable side of Jewish settlement in Poland, Lithuania and a host of countries and provinces in the East had been dominant, in effect, until a century before the Gaon's time. The specific drive eastward into Poland had taken place in the 13th century in the wake of Tartar invasions which had devastated the country, leaving huge territories open for settlement and colonisation. German merchants and craftsmen were invited in warmly by Polish rulers, and Jews were specifically included with guarantees of safety and freedom of worship.

Despite Church hostility, they were soon producing a rapidly increasing population in Poland and Lithuania. Those with special talents found their way into securing leases from the nobles as administrators or partners of land and forest development under what became known as the "Arenda" system. Large tracts of land were allotted by the nobles for the establishment of "private cities," free of urban controls, and with supplies of building materials for houses and synagogues. Though the drive east had come mainly from central Europe, where the Jews were desperate to get away from persecution during the Crusades and in the period of the Black Death. Jewish settlements included large migration from the Khazar land of Asia Minor, and from a variety of other countries under Byzantine control. This included many Sephardi Jews, who clung, as usual, to their own forms of worship and *halachic* (legal) law.

But behind the variety, their common faith and their Yiddish language provided a strong uniformity, creating a civilisation unique in Jewish history. A decisive extension had come in the 16th century when the huge steppes of the Ukraine had come under the rule of Polish nobles, after the 1569 Union of Brest-Litovsk, with many Jews put in charge as administrators of agriculture and forests and for organising the work of the serfs. Inevitably, the patriotic rising in 1648 against Polish rule singled out the Jews as scapegoats, with massacres that were epochal in their intensity. Yet even after this decisive shock to Jewish security, the underlying pattern of Jewish existence remained in being, with leading Jews maintaining leasehold privileges, operating as tax-farmers, providing finance for development, and being extremely active in international trade both with Western Europe and eastward with Russia proper. Below this privileged level, the great mass of Jews fashioned a difficult but often satisfying existence; and in the *shtetl*, which offered the most characteristic social innovation for the Jews over the vast areas of Eastern Europe, there was always a *gvir* (a substantial citizen) who exercised great responsibility not only in helping individual Jews, but as a intermediary with non-Jewish authorities at all levels.

The thing that has been is the thing that will be again.

Ecclesiastes

Within this broad picture the Jews had developed their own forms of self-government in a graduated series of Councils, with leadership defined in constitutional forms that covered both rabbinic and secular authority and culminated at the top level in a major "Council of Four Lands." These Councils held their sessions where Jews met at the great fairs—such as Lublin and Jaroslav—with the intermediate days of Passover as a favoured time. There were major economic issues to be discussed, covering both internal *halachic* questions on which argument had arisen locally, and the assessment and collection of taxes for which they were held responsible. The overall unity of these vast areas did not rule out local "patriotic" loyalties, many of which were handed on to later generations. "Litvaks" (Lithuanians, of whom I am one) were encouraged to feel intellectually superior to "Polacks," who in turn felt (probably correctly) more imaginative than their prosaic rivals; and though all spoke Yiddish, there were very distinctive accents and vocabularies.

In considering the Gaon's era as a turning point, it is relevant that it was in his lifetime that far-reaching changes were superimposed politically, with Czarist Russia suddenly dominant in a new way,

86

in consequence of the Partitions of Poland between major European Powers—Russia, Austria and Prussia—that began in 1772. The immediate consequence was the allotment of lands with large Jewish populations to these Powers, the major instance of which was the huge Jewish population that fell under Russian control. The Russian Government was determined to prevent these Jews from having a free run into Russia proper, and forbade their moving beyond a strict "Pale of Settlement." As time went on, the political domination by Russia of this major part of the Jewish world put a new kind of blight on any existing sense of freedom, creating a long-lasting sense of "Russian oppression" for many generations among all descendants of the East European world.

Jews were always men . . . who have fought and suffered on every battle field of human thought.

HEINRICH
HEINE

Yet within this one is aware, with hindsight, that the era which followed the Gaon was receptive in some ways to some liberating Russian influences. The ban on the residence or movement of Jews "beyond the Pale" was never absolute in practice: there were valuable privileges to be won in the Russian orbit by those who displayed great economic initiative, superior to what would have been the less opportunistic worlds of Poland and the Baltic States. Beneath the surface, too, the Russian world opened doors ultimately in the cultural field. One always has to allow for a to-and-fro in Jewish history; and if we see the Gaon's lifetime as pointing, in one sense, towards a future "westernization," we note at the same time that the growth in the strength of the Hasidic following moved in the opposite direction, and was for this reason fiercely opposed by the Gaon when it tried to establish itself in his domain of Vilna.

The Hebrew word *"Hasid"* means "gracious." The essence of the new movement, which had taken root in remote Podolia in the early part of the 18th century, lay in a celebration of the joy of worship and a fervent allegiance in all matters to those chosen as *rebbes* (masters) whose quasi-magical intense mystical exercises signifies closeness to God. The Gaon may have welcomed the piety of these *rebbes*; but where Hasidism led to individuals surrendering moral responsibility for their own lives and subjecting themselves, however happily, to the instructions of a *rebbe*, it was, in his view, akin to paganism.

Where Hasidism led to individuals surrendering moral responsibility for their own lives and subjecting themselves, however happily, to the instructions of a *rebbe*, it was, in his view, akin to paganism.

Hasidism had grown from the charismatic teachings of a wandering "miracle-worker," a familiar character in peasant life, dispensing remedies and charms and known among the Jews as a *baal shem*, a title meaning "Master of the Name," or more correctly "the God-Man." This particular *baal shem* had instilled affection and respect to such a degree that he was known as *baal shem tov*, "the good God-Man." The love of God which he instilled was permeated by an evident sense of joy. In the early phase of Hasidism, the love of learning became less important than the joy of worship and the love of the *rebbe*, an approach which automatically won the Gaon's disapproval.

Our laws have been such as have always inspired admiration and imitation in all other men.

JOSEPHUS

There was little opposition to this form of worship and piety as Hasidism spread through Volhynnia and towards the Gaon's centre in Vilna. Anticipating the Gaon's opposition to anything which derogated study, a number of scholars tried to broaden the Hasidic base by expounding kabbalistic teaching in the framework of the new approach. One particular Hasidic rabbi, called Shneur Zalman of Lyady, wrote a highly intellectual book known as *Tanya* with this purpose in mind, but sought in vain to have discussions with the Gaon to get his ideas considered. Far from this, the Gaon issued a letter banning Hasidism in all the areas he could reach. Passions rose, with appeals to the non-Jewish authorities, excommunications, and court cases. To the Gaon's followers, it was *his* authority, stemming from the high reaches of his learning, which had to be respected, but nothing could heal the rift. Communal strife denigrated into unswerving mutual hatred, leaving echoes years later among the descendants of the different groups.

In this conflict of views, one sees again how the Gaon's era was to some extent a cross-road of the many strands in Jewish life. In one broad sense, it might seem clear that what one might call the Litvak respect for reason, which flowed from him, became dominant, as Jews entered Western life more fully; but we have seen in our time a strengthening of some of the strands which were linked to the Hasidim, and for which he had no patience. In most cases this is only a minor historical remnant, which surfaces as a strong allegiance by devoted but small number of followers to the hereditary *rebbes* of long surviving "clans" of Hasidim; but more significantly there has been a remarkable growth of one Hasidic group, the Lubavitch movement, which in the Gaon's day was promoted by the scholarly rabbi, Shneur Zalman of Lyady, whom the Gaon tried so hard to outlaw. In religious action, the Lubavitch movement is engaged in a passionate promotion—or recovery—of Jewish faith and practice, and is expanding everywhere. Here, too, the hereditary or selected leader of this large movement is venerated with religious intensity; and it is significant that Shneur Zalman's book *Tanya* is used as an eloquent text for an expression of the domain of the transcendent in Jewish religious thought.

To some extent this development is in line with the strengthening of fundamentalist thought everywhere, and in the Jewish case drawing deeply on *kabbalah* and other aspects of Jewish tradition. It is unexpected that one group of Hasidim have expanded so strongly to strengthen the Jewish faith. The Gaon might well have been surprised, but perhaps not entirely displeased.

When will God give me leave to go up and make my home within the extolled gates of Zion.

SHALEM SHABAZI, Yemen, 17th c.

VIII

SIR MOSES MONTEFIORE

1784–1895

A 19th-century Palestine Jew in the finery of dress that includes a tall Sephardi hat and fur-lined pelisse, with trousers of pale silk, and little Morocco slippers.

W E H A V E already seen in this book that the Jewish faith has been expressed in a vast variety of forms throughout history; but we have also been made aware that these different forms are pervaded by an underlying continuum which brings all the different forms together. A potent example arises when we turn from the East European world of the Vilna Gaon to that of the distinguished Englishman Sir Moses Montefiore. As it happens, Montefiore's work for the Jewish people was heavily concerned with the Jewish masses of Central and Eastern Europe, and the underlying unity becomes all the more remarkable in the contrast of the two worlds.

Staying for a moment with the contrast, the Vilna Gaon, as we saw in the last chapter, was an outstanding scholar who lived his life in something close to poverty, pursuing his biblical and rabbinic studies through the night in isolation, never needing normally to turn from his Jewish studies to raise any political issues with leaders of the non-Jewish world around him. At the other extreme, Montefiore, growing into a man of great wealth and influence, was totally at home with political leaders of many countries, using these contacts to promote a never-ending series of programmes aimed at improving the welfare throughout the world of Jews suffering from the persecutions of that time. Whereas the Vilna Gaon turned to the non-Jewish world with the utmost reluctance and only when some direct religious principle seemed involved—as when he felt that the rapid spread of Hasidism had to be held back from becoming too dominant in Jewish life, Sir Moses Montefiore drew eagerly on his wealth and intimate friendship with Queen Victoria to harness the support of Governments everywhere to redress Jewish wrongs.

The contrast seems all-embracing, which makes the common ground of these two historical figures all the more stimulating. At the most obvious level, a basic parallel in their lives is that both men evinced an unshakeable faith in their Jewish heritage, expressed in both cases in a scrupulous observance of traditional religious practices. In simple religious terms, the affirmation of the *Shema* (Hear, O Israel, the Lord our God is One) was, one might say, the ultimate expression for both men of their Jewish religious faith.

But this is only part of the continuum that we have been exploring in this book. It is as symbols of the underlying force of Jewish history that the linkage of their lives is so striking. Each was uniquely poised to express this. With the Gaon's life, 1720 to 1797, covering the major part of the 18th century, he was contemporary with an approaching turning-point of Jewish experience, obscure at the time but very visible with hindsight. As a traditionalist, it was his nature to fight off every kind of modernism, particularly in the Enlightenment ideas beginning to surface among some German Jews; yet change was in the background, recognised in some of his own intellectual ideas and vivified towards the end of his life by the French Revolution. The political upheavals that were intensified in the Napoleonic era were to bring both benefits and tragedies to Jewish life in the stirrings of nationalisms.

For the time being, however, the outstanding factor in the Jewish world lay in the remarkable rise in the Jewish populations of Central and Eastern Europe, carried forward with even greater intensity in the 19th century to develop into the overpowering heartland of Jewish life. Here, perhaps unexpectedly, is the strongest link with the 19th century work of Montefiore. For though his first foray, in 1840, into his life-long role as the ambassador of Jewish life was centered on the Jews of Damascus, most of his work later was increasingly targeted towards the rapidly mounting persecutions of Eastern Europe.

The background to this emphasis in his work is immediately clear when one looks at population figures. A new balance in Jewish life had taken shape from the 16th century on. Until then, Sephardi Jews of the South and East had constituted the majority of Jews of the world; but from then on, for a combination of political and economic reasons, the Ashkenazi Jews of Northern and Eastern Europe had grown into the overwhelming majority. Population scholars calculate that by 1820 there were more than one and one-half-million Jews in Russia plus some 650,000 in Austria-Hungary and Rumania, while Sephardi Jews around the Mediterranean totalled no more than 300,000. By the end of the 19th century this shift had become even more pronounced. The figure for Russia and Poland had grown to some 5.2 million, with Austria-Hungary and Rumania adding another 2.3 million. For comparison, there were less than 20,000 Jews in England at the beginning of the 19th century, growing to no more than 300,000 by the end of the century. It is, of course, all the more remarkable that Montefiore, as leader of this tiny community, was able to exercise strong influence throughout the world, startling in itself until one sees it in the context of Britain's strong industrial and financial dominance for a large part of Montefiore's century.

The Bible has been the Magna Carta of the poor and of the oppressed.

T.H. HUXLEY, 1892

Yet this broad economic picture is only part of the explanation for the carrying power of Montefiore's influence. Looking for a fuller reason, one starts by recognising elements in his own character, manifest in the strength of his religious convictions, and echoed significantly by his dignified physique: he was a man of 6.3 feet in height. As so often elsewhere, the personal factors in history seem to outweigh the broad factors with which one is more usually concerned; and here the details are full of interest in their own right. One sees in them how it was that Montefiore was able to enjoy the distinctive pride that he drew from his Sephardi background while at the same time acting in full concert with leading Ashkenazi Jews like the Rothschilds, who had in any case become closely connected to him by marriage.

But if Montefiore's special role in Jewish history can be linked largely to these details of the time and place of his life, it bears the mark also of factors in England's island story that were all-important to his influence. England's relationship with the Jews had already shown characteristics different from elsewhere. For one thing, Jews had left virtually no mark on the English scene for some 500 years after their expulsion in 1191; and as a result, there was little active hostility to some quiet infiltration when circumstances made it a natural development. This situation arose when a few Jews with special trading and financial expertise found their way to England after the expulsions from Spain and Portugal in the 1490s. Some also began to come less directly from Turkey and Italy, followed later by Sephardim who had settled in South America and the Caribbean.

Another positive factor was the religious background in England. This had become very sympathetic to the Jews when the Protestant faith tightened its hold on English life during the reign of Queen Elizabeth and her successor King James. A major factor in this was the availability of the Bible in the magnificent 1611 translation which became known as the King James, or the Authorised, Version. If some of this biblical fervour was softened by less-principled attitudes in the 18th century, it was more than restored in the 19th through the moral style generated by the reign of Queen Victoria. This provided an extremely friendly background for the moral appeal to the British public of Montefiore's tireless efforts to relieve the persecutions suffered in many countries by the People of the Book.

In all these ways, it could be said, Montefiore's presence in England in the 19th century was a rendezvous with history. Stepping outside the general factors that we have touched on, we have to allow also for a remarkable "accident": that he lived and worked beneficently for the Jews throughout a life that lasted more than 100 years (1784–1885), and that Queen Victoria, also very long-lived (1819– 1901), had a close friendship with him for more than fifty of these years.

The Queen undoubtedly warmed particularly to the Jewish aspects of his work. The honour of his early knighthood as one of the two Sheriffs of London in 1838 was upgraded by her in a much more personal way eight years later when she conferred on him the hereditary title of baronet, in her hope, the Prime Minister told him, "that it may aid your truly beneficent efforts to improve the social conditions of the Jews in other countries by temperate appeals to the justice and humanity of their rulers."

The Queen's approach reflected the widespread admiration throughout the country for the arduous negotiations he undertook year by year after his first mission to Egypt in 1840 over the Damascus "Blood Libel." His aim in this case was to secure the release of Jews facing death sentences after the monstrous accusation that they had killed a Catholic priest and his servant to obtain blood "needed to bake Passover matzah." After intense effort, Montefiore persuaded the Sultan of Turkey, head of Islam, to declare to the Moslem world in an official *firman* that this allegation had absolutely no justification.

We Jews have a more pressing responsibility for our lives and beliefs than perhaps any other religious community.

C.G. MONTEFIORE

It was the first of his triumphs, and it elicited the Queen's special admiration. Historically, a number of other Jews had long been awarded royal honours in England, but always for their *general* work for the country. As an example, the immigrant Solomon de Medina, had been knighted in the early 1700's for financing and victualling the victorious armies of the great Duke of Marlborough, ancestor of Winston Churchill. In Victoria's own reign, the banker Gold-smid had been created a baronet seven years before Montefiore, but here too without the intimate respect that the Queen felt for Montefiore's Jewish work.

But though this establishes the unique side of Montefiore's national and international fame, it in no way detracts from his more general role as a leader in Britain's financial and industrial society, a base he needed, indeed, for the immense and costly missions he was ready to undertake. From early youth he had worked very hard in this field, with such success that by the age of forty he was free to take the decision to give up all his active business work so that he could devote virtually all his time and resources to helping his people wherever they needed him.

The elements in his speedy rise to financial independence are by themselves a vivid illustration of how a small number of inter-connected Jewish families in north-west Europe contributed creatively to England's emerging dominance in this period. Initially, one thinks of it as a Sephardi story, since it was through the expulsions from Spain and Portugal that a long-lasting base was established in England in trade and finance. But while this aspect will always have special interest in relation to Sephardi nostalgia, the full picture is dominated more heavily by the early presence of Ashkenazi-German qualities and potentialities.

Montefiore's own background is a perfect illustration. If we were looking particularly at the Sephardi side, we would note that his grandfather, a Sephardi merchant of Leghorn (Italy) had a family link with the English Sir Solomon de Medina, mentioned earlier. Montefiore's father in turn married a Mocatta of the famous banking family which had settled in England as early as the 17th century. More positively, however, it was the Ashkenazi financial leadership

A Jewish lady of Gibraltar, in her 19th-century Eastern-Oriental attire.

which made its mark when Britain was in the throes of the 18th century colonial and Napoleonic wars in which victory was to lay the foundations of imperial power. Far the most important figure in this process was an Ashkenazi immigrant from Holland called Levy Barent Cohen; and here we see very neatly the dynastic background to Montefiore's emergence. One of Cohen's daughters married the first English Rothschild; a second daughter married Montefiore.

But once again, a factual analysis of the story yields only part of its meaning. Certainly the close links with the swiftly rising Rothschilds was all-important financially. Montefiore was stockbroker to the Rothschilds during the early 19th century decades which witnessed the phenomenal rise of this great merchant bank, and he participated to the full in the many international developments—for example in mining, gas installation and insurance—which were financed from England during this boom period. But if he was skilled in business, it is really as an incurable romantic that the story of his life has to be told.

The pivot of this feeling was his love of the ancestral land, "the Holy Land," as he saw it, central to his inner feeling as a Jew. He and his wife made their first pilgrimage there in 1827, shortly after his retirement from full-time business. It was the first of his seven visits, in each of which he combined his vivid sense of veneration with tireless efforts to promote the welfare of the Jews living there, mostly in abject poverty.

Palestine was currently under Turkish control, but with a small British governmental presence aimed particularly at offering some "protection" to Jews, to match in a small way the "protection" provided to Catholics by the French, and to the Greek Orthodox by the Russians. Far ahead of his time, Montefiore sought to help the Jews living there not simply with financial and agricultural help but also with plans to modernize their very primitive industry. Among many practical projects, he set out to improve their housing by building a terrace of small cottages outside the walls of the Old City, which survive today in beautifully restored form as a very

With the Synagogue began a new type of worship in the history of humanity.

Rev. Travers Herford, 1930

appropriate memorial to his life's work there. He himself defined the nature of his feeling in an interview he gave in 1863 when he was nearly eighty. When asked what he felt about the restoration of Jews to the Holy Land, he said:

> It was my constant dream. I do not expect that all Israelites will quit their abodes, but Palestine must belong to the Jews, with Jerusalem destined to be the seat of a Jewish empire.

With Jews everywhere his concern, he accepted a constant responsibility in Britain itself to keep the Jewish community hard at work over all religious and social issues arising there. To this end he not only led the ancient Sephardi community, but as President for many years of the Board of Deputies of British Jews, he also brought Sephardim and Ashkenazim together for wider work. This was particularly important when news would reach England of some particularly cruel persecutions overseas, calling for "rescue missions," usually led by Montefiore himself.

In a volume published in 1985 to celebrate the double anniversaries of his birth and death, one contributor, Professor Ursula Henriques, scion herself of an old Sephardi family, offers a graphic description of the methods and range of these numerous journeys:

> Sir Moses' method of going about these rescue missions was well established. He prepared the ground by making contact with as many representatives and important ministers of the country concerned as could be reached. He then secured promises of support from the rulers of other European powers. Next he obtained letters of introduction (readily granted by successive British Foreign Ministers) to the British ambassadors and consuls in the area. Finally he collected a band of fellow travellers, and set out.

> Invariably he went straight to the top. He sought and obtained interviews with the Sultan of Turkey, with Mehmet Ali, the rebellious Pasha of Egypt, (Czar) Nicholas I of Russia, Louis Napoleon of Paris, and Queen Isabella of Spain, en route to Marrakesh, where he was formally entertained by the Sultan.

Those parts of his voluminous diaries which were published after his death bring out in detail the arduous nature of these journeys, which were wider in range than in the list above. In every place visited, he brought up the crippling disabilities suffered by the Jews, and argued strongly with the heads of the Governments concerned that State announcements should abolish these persecutions. The detail is illuminating in other ways, too. In his visit to Rumania in 1867, his warm reception by Prince Carol was offset by virulent attacks by local antisemites. Facing a hostile crowd surrounding his hotel in Bucharest, he threw open his room windows and addressed the rioters fearlessly. In an important visit to Morocco at the age of eighty, his negotiations for imprisoned Jews helped British policy through an agreement which brought a long-standing British-Spanish dispute on Morocco to an end. On his first visit to Russia in 1846 (he went again in 1872 at the age of eighty-eight), he was able during his return journey to spend eleven days with the enthusiastic Jewish community of Vilna, and showed his respect for their legendary leader the Gaon of Vilna (discussed in the last chapter) by visiting his tomb there.

. . . and that idleness is the door to temptation and sin.

Chief Rabbi Hertz, 1935

His reception in Vilna, and later in Warsaw, was typical of the extraordinary enthusiasm that his work aroused all over the Jewish world. This was paralleled in England itself by the warm respect of the general public, evinced in packed meetings of support at the Mansion House, and many commendatory articles in the British Press.

Most appropriately, perhaps, one finds in *The Times* of October 23, 1883, his anniversary year, a long editorial, couched in Victorian terms, which offers an apt exposition both of his contribution to England and to the pride of his own people.

Central to the argument of the article is a recognition of the immense changes to his own country and the world at large during his "immense age"; but with great insight the writer also sees Montefiore as one of the great figures of Jewish history:

> The people for whom he has done so much do him honour for the work of helping his suffering brethren wherever they are to be found. His journeys to Palestine began in 1827, and they only ended in 1875 when he was past ninety years of age. . . .

But what distinguishes the work of Sir Moses Montefiore from that of any other philanthropist is the success with which he has pleaded the cause of the Jews in the quarters to which, under ordinary circumstances, their cry could not have reached. . . .

It could be said that Montefiore's presence in England in the 19th century was a rendezvous with history.

Twenty years earlier, a leading article in the London *Jewish Chronicle* had expressed the feeling of the Jews themselves as Sir Moses announced that he was leaving for Morocco to rescue Jews there who had been falsely accused of murder:

> Once again, the most illustrious son of the Patriarchs must gird up his loins, a man approaching eighty . . . We tremble for so precious a life. But since the mission has arisen, let us confess that no co-religionist all over the globe is so well qualified as Israel's veteran champion.

Remembering his past . . . Invariably he went straight to the top.
He sought and obtained interviews with the Sultan of Turkey.

IX

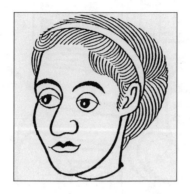

EMMA LAZARUS

1849–1887

Emma Lazarus was drawn into a passionate involvement with those Jews from Eastern Europe who had begun to stream into America.

IT MAY BE surprising that Emma Lazarus, virtually unknown to most people except as the author of a few lines of verse, is put forward here to express through her life one of the most dramatic developments ever seen in Jewish history. This can be summed up as the almost magical transformation of the poverty-stricken Jewish millions of the United States, and all within a few brief decades. Every aspect of this transformation, in cultural as well as in economic terms, is tangible in her life.

Emma Lazarus was born in New York in 1849 and died, at less than forty, in 1887. In this short life, she expressed not simply the birth-pangs of the new American-Jewish experience but the major historical movements that preceded it and those which were to follow. In this sense her life reaches back and forward in a unique way.

A clue to this can be found in the lines of verse for which she is always remembered. Her early literary work, which led to friendship with Emerson and Longfellow, was gentle and inward-looking, but in the 1880's, only a few years before she died, she was suddenly drawn into a passionate involvement with those Jews from Eastern Europe who had begun to stream into America in order to escape from the effects of an outbreak of pogroms, adding to the poverty and discrimination from which they already suffered. One expression by her of America's role in receiving the new inflow of refugees was a sonnet in which she saw prophetically that this was not to be a brief episode but a major transforming process, in which the massive numbers involved led to the creation of a new Jewish civilisation. Twenty years after she wrote this sonnet, the lines were engraved on a plaque which was fixed to the base of the Statue of Liberty which had been erected on the landing centre of Ellis Island in New York Harbour. The one line which is always remembered expresses it all: "Give me your tired, your poor, your huddled masses yearning to breathe free."

She had in fact begun to do welfare work for refugees in general before the Jewish explosion; and she had also awakened to the significance of her Jewish roots before the arrival *en masse* of East European Jews brought everything together in a new form. What

A Jew is never an applicant for public or private charity outside of Judaism . . .

Editorial,
Philadelphia,
1872

107

is dramatized in her lines is the potential bounty for all humanity of the transcending welcome that America offered. America, in her words, was Mother of Exiles: "From her beacon-hand glows world-wide welcome." Yet though unspoken in the sonnet, she was undoubtedly thinking of the intense application of this new force to the salvation of her own people.

For some years before this, Emma's exploration of the meaning of being Jewish had been mainly cultural in form. She had found herself stirred by the ideas on Jewish cultural history expressed in George Eliot's remarkable novel *Daniel Deronda*. Pursuing this, she had used a German version of Hebrew poetry written in the "Golden Age" of Spain—Judah Halevi and Solomon ibn Gabirol—to produce her own translations of these poets, side-by-side with essays, novels and dramas on many Jewish themes. It was the stream of refugees that provided her now with a double base for her thoughts on being Jewish. In this vein she formulated, shortly before her death, a wholly original view that went far beyond the middle-class Jewish outlook that surrounded her. Jewish life, she wrote, must depend for the future on the twin centres of America and Palestine.

In Russia itself, the despair generated by the pogroms had led many thinkers to see the Jewish future solely in terms of a return to the ancestral land. A new movement expressing this called *Hibbat Zion* (love of Zion) had aroused enormous enthusiasm, and become an inspiration vital for those willing to confront the insuperable problems of settlement in Palestine. The future American role in this was, as yet, quite unforseen. The number of Jews in the United States was still very small, probably less than 300,000. That it would grow by the end of the century to a million, and continue to expand in numbers and Jewish feeling for decades to come was not a reality for the *Hibbat Zion* pioneers; and yet without this, the miracle of the creation of the State of Israel would never have happened.

Before America took over Jewish world leadership, the creation of a tolerable life for the teeming millions of Eastern European and other impoverished areas had been led by the Jewish aristocracy of Western Europe, exemplified above all, as we saw in the last chapter, by the extraordinary personal position of Sir Moses Montefiore. For religious reasons deeply felt, he had tried to improve physical conditions for the scattering of Jews who lived in the Holy Land, but the main props of his work had been a search for civil rights and physical safety in countries denying this to Jews. By itself this might seem a narrow approach, without much future. More correctly, however, it has to be seen as a historical breakthrough in which Jews of privilege reached out in a wholly new way to help the oppressed masses. It is only by comparison with the American century to follow that the limitations of political pleading in the 19th century become so apparent.

There is a vast storehouse filled with treasures. The key: the Hebrew language . . .

HENRIETTA SZOLD, 1896

It was by instinct that Emma felt the possibilities of American leadership. Even in the few words of her sonnet, one can see how she grasped the significance of her moment in history. It became clear in the decades which were to follow, but it would never have been a natural development unless the earlier history of the Jews in America had provided a background bringing together some of the many strands embodied in what we have called the Jewish "continuum." Because some of these strands lay to hand in the varied experiences of Emma Lazarus's own life, she could forsee the future in terms of the double setting that she regarded as inevitable.

To understand these sources and their significance for the future, one has to see the early history of American Jewry in three phases. In the first, covering the 17th–18th centuries, such leadership as emerged was heavily Sephardi in character. In the second phase, starting around 1825, there was a rapidly expanding immigration of Jews from various German-speaking countries in Europe, Ashkenazi by definition, but following their faith in what one might call a relaxed German-Protestant style, and to this extent prompted by much of the simple but comfortable background they had left behind. In the third phase, beginning in the 1880s with the inflow of Yiddish-speaking Jews from an intensely Jewish background, a wholly new style began to be forged, hesitant at first yet fertile in promise. It is because the world of Emma Lazarus had a direct relation to all three phases that we can see her as a symbolic forerunner of the unitary American-Jewish approach that was to emerge, after much travail, in the dramatic century that was to follow.

The first strand in Emma's life was her very positive Sephardi origin. Given the dominance later of the two successive inflows, German and Yiddish, one can easily omit to note how distinctive and long-lasting the Sephardi phase had been. It was always relevant that the story of American Jewry began when twenty-three Sephardi refugees from the former Dutch area of Brazil stepped ashore in New Amsterdam (New York to be) in September 1654 and were grudgingly permitted to stay on because of a ruling by the governing Dutch West India Company. It was this Sephardi base which continued to exercise its influence long after Ashkenazi Jews began to arrive. The Sephardi style and rituals were adopted for a long time when synagogues opened, strengthened by continuing contacts with Sephardis in England and Caribbean islands.

Two of Emma's great-grandparents had arrived from the Caribbean at around the time of the American Revolution. It was a period in which well-educated Sephardi rabbis drawn from Europe as well as Caribbean sources felt free to participate in the burgeoning political development in their new world. There is an apt illustration in the career of Rabbi Gershom Mendes Seixas, *Haham* of the original prestigious Sephardi synagogue in New York. Having shown support for Washington, he was invited to the Inauguration and subsequently became a Trustee of Columbia College in New York, where his portrait now hangs.

Emma's father had a substantial business in New York as a sugar refiner and distiller. Family life was conducted on privileged lines: he saw to it that Emma was educated at home by private tutors, with an emphasis on languages—French, German and Italian, all extremely significant later in her literary work. Yet though the Sephardi origin still yielded a special kind of pride to some old families, the socio-economic background to Emma's world now drew more significantly on the growing prosperity and self-confidence that had been engendered swiftly during what we noted as the "second phase" of Jewish-American history, in the early decades of the 19th century.

The fascination that this period exercises arises partly because it was linked to the era in which the somewhat encrusted experience of colonial times was transformed by the opening up of American life on a vastly expanded stage. Dramatically, this heralded the future by bringing the Far West fully into the picture for the first time; but infinitely more interesting at this stage was the opening up to a new life of all the huge areas between the East and West Coasts.

It was here that American Jewry really took off, finding a highly successful role through the ability of the enterprising German-Jewish immigrants to rise to their new opportunities, responding to needs that had to be met as part of the expansion of economic settlement. The functions of the Jews engaged in this were certainly modest and undramatic for quite a time; but as part of a highly mobile society they were soon seen as essential in what they did, ingenious, palpably honest, and infusing even basic activities of peddling and shopkeeping with a host of ancillary occupations. They were soon forming small but stable communities everywhere, distinctive yet accepted, and in many cases laying a basis, as their functions expanded, for the emergence later of some of the great American fortunes.

Much of this process had made its mark by the middle of the 19th century. With individual enterprise essential, the new immigrants had often by-passed the old colonial cities where Jews already lived to settle at first in more virgin territory along the Mississippi and Ohio Rivers and the Great Lakes. The larger part remained heavily concentrated in the North Eastern States, though the diffusion extended all the way to California.

If this was for many a volatile kind of life, it was anchored both to Jewish loyalties and the legacy of German culture that remained potent in social, as well as in literary and musical terms. In time, the German link gave way to involvement with more generalized European ideas that Jews absorbed within the American background they were now exploring. As part of the same adjustment process many were eager to respond to a more modern expression of Jewish ritual, half akin in style to the Protestant world of America. Reform Judaism, with "Temples" as dignified as churches, spread everywhere. To the rising Jewish bourgeois, the history that had produced the rigid orthodoxies of Eastern Europe was no longer

Whither shall they turn? for the West hath cast them out, and the East refuseth to receive.

EMMA LAZARUS: *The Exodus*

III

Give me your tired, your poor, your huddled masses yearning to breathe free, the wretched refuse of your teeming shore, send these, the homeless, tempest-tossed, to me: I lift my lamp beside the Golden Door.

relevant. Emma Lazarus felt stirred to identify with this world; but for many it seemed natural to assume that the old links of kith and kin no longer applied in democratic America.

Prosperity triggered the first upset to this view. Having enjoyed a good deal of respect as they made their way, in their own style, up the economic ladder, many were disconcerted to find in the 1870s that the social elite were determined to keep them at a distance. Even Reform Jews, fully modern in style and contributing generously to welfare and the arts, would not find the door open. The American dream clearly had some built-in ambivalence.

There is a tiny but vivid illustration, related pointedly to the world of Emma herself, in a fascinating book: *A Documentary History of the Jews in the United States*. The editor, Professor Morris U. Schappes, includes a newly discovered letter, written in November 1863 in New York, to the Christian clergyman Rev. H.W. Bellows who had been put in charge of a campaign to raise funds to take care of sick and wounded soldiers (and their families) fighting in the Civil War. A great "Metropolitan Fair" was being organised in New York with stalls manned by volunteers of all religions. A Jewish committee, anxious to cooperate, had urged at first that there should be a Jewish stall, looked after by "pretty Jewesses"; and this was agreed. Then the Jews changed their minds, telling Bellows that they had decided against a separate Jewish stall. Volunteers were not to be identified in religious terms. At a similar Fair held in Rochester (New York) the Jewish Committee stated, like the New York City Committee, that "the only national character in which they wished to appear would be under the Star Spangled Banner." Professor Schappes notes drily that though there were no Jewish stalls anywhere, there were Episcopalian, Lutheran, Baptist, Methodist, Presbyterian and Dutch Reformed Church stalls. He adds: "Thus the Jewish middle-class interpretation of equality had led to effacement."

Emma, so deeply concerned with the historic meaning of being Jewish, may well have noted the timidity of the Jews around her. We see in further notes that her father Morris was an active member of the Jewish Men's Committee, with his sister-in-law working on the Ladies Committee. Other names mentioned are heavily German (Ein-

I am an example of the universality of our claims for not only American women . . . for I am a daughter of . . . the persecuted people, the Jews.

Rights of Women, 1852

stein, Seligman, Bernheimer and others) evoking the rich Jews of *Our Crowd* and the exclusions that *they* faced. The ease of the formative period had gone. The Jews now realised that even the heaviest contributions to welfare and the arts would not get them through the doors that mattered, in clubs, hotels, the top universities, and so on. It was not until well after World War II—at least 80 years later—that the exclusion bars were no longer universal.

Yet within this time, the emergence of American Jewry as the greatest Jewish community the world had ever seen had moved forward with an extraordinary momentum. To some extent, history had demanded it. The transformation of the earlier Jewish society was conditioned by the needs of the Jewish masses of Eastern Europe, desperate for refuge. Yet it could never have been accomplished without the historic liberalism of American life and its limitless economic potential. Here, too, the story unfolded in phases, each presenting a challenge that seemed insuperable, and each offering a response in due course which transcended earlier expectations.

In the first challenge, Emma Lazarus herself, it could be said, set the signals correctly. From the beginning she had responded to the unity within Jewish history, in contrast to those of her contemporaries whose aim was to live within their own horizons, and wanted nothing to do with the "primitive" masses streaming in from Eastern Europe. It took time before the comfortably placed "uptown" Jews expanded their minimum welfare work for the immigrants into well-organised programmes of work, health and education; but this became the process that took over, and within a generation or two the emerging immigrants were increasingly poised to add to the Jewish community, and to America itself, their own contributions of enterprise and intelligence.

The shock of their arrival had given way to a new appreciation of unexplored values feeding into American life. Variety was still the essence, but it began to be regarded as axiomatic that all Jews shared some responsibility. Increasingly there was a palpable sense of unity between the varied segments of American Jewish life.

Emma's instinct had been justified. In all the subsequent dramas of

The Jews are the intensive form . . . of any nationality whose language and customs they adopt.

EMMA
LAZARUS

114

the 20th century, an underlying sense of common purpose grew stronger with each challenge. This is not to say that deep argument was overcome. But the ultimate realities of the Holocaust and Israel revealed that at this level an indestructible unity permeated the thoughts and endeavours of this huge community.

Emma Lazarus had foreseen the joint roles of America and Israel in expressing the continuum of Jewish history. It is a story of constant enrichment in new forms, and Emma has a deserved place in the *minyan* of those who have given it character.

Belonging to a people known as the Veterans of History, *puts serious responsibility on our shoulders.*

S.M. DUBNOW, 1893

Jews filled the sweat shops of the garment industry.

115

X

CHAIM WEIZMANN

1874–1952

It was in student years that he threw himself into Zionism . . . in night-long arguments with communists and non-Zionist socialists.

To HAVE BEEN a Jew during the middle years of the 20th century means to have lived through an era which was, at the same time, the most horrifying and the most inspiring in Jewish history. The dominating events—the Holocaust on the one hand, and the creation of Israel on the other—dwarf everything that had gone before. To find a single figure, as I have done in the earlier chapters of this book, who somehow symbolises in his or her own person, a sustaining force in the faith that Jews carried with them through these awesome events, might seem an insuperable task. But there is one person who can satisfy that demand: a Jew born in 1874 in a *shtetl* (village) called Motol in Eastern Europe, who went on to play a leading role in transforming the Jewish history of our time. He was the scientist and Jewish leader Chaim Weizmann.

The handful of Zionists and their descendants are changing the entire future of mankind.

J.H. HERTZ, 1917

There is of course a difference between looking at figures of the past who are now purely historical, and someone of our own time, whom many remember personally, perhaps with criticism as well as admiration. But it is more than a difference of objectivity which makes it hard to choose one person who can epitomise the story of this century. When we call on someone to help us to express the emotional legacy of the Holocaust—the cold-blooded murder of millions of Jews—we are looking not just for facts but for something like solace. Weizmann's achievements are matters of record; but I choose him above all for the *quality* of his vision. He had an unfaltering sense of principle, which he drew from the Bible and his childhood origins, and which we in turn can draw on, to help us to live with the enormity of what happened. Not that Weizmann was a saintly character in everything he did. We have, as it happens, a unique way of judging him as a person through a huge collection of letters published in some twenty-five volumes, stretching from a letter he wrote at the age of eleven, to the last letter before his death in 1952, as President of Israel. Throughout his life, and especially in his early years as an impoverished research chemist, writing letters all over Europe, and all through the night, to whip up enthusiasm for a Jewish Homeland, he is passionate, aggressive, sarcastic and relentless; yet at the same time the idealism within him is always paramount, expressed to friends with warmth and tenderness, laced frequently with a coruscating wit. The letters are, in fact, a documented illustration of the strength of character that everyone who met him recognized instantly. It was this quality that won the support, at vital moments, of political leaders like Churchill, who were inspired by his vision of Jews being allowed to return to their ancestral land after two thousand years in exile.

There is one sense in which Weizmann is an exemplar of our time in a more familiar way. Untold numbers of Jews emerged in our century, as Weizmann did, from the isolation of "Shtetl" existence to full participation in western life. For many, this mixed background often presented problems of acceptance. What was remarkable about Weizmann was that he made it his aim, from his earliest youth, to turn the folk-warmth of his ancestral religion into a pride that would sustain a free and equal partnership with the non-Jewish world. He was, in a word, the most inward-looking and the most outward-looking Jew that anyone ever met. But a balance within himself was not enough. The Jewish masses of Russia had to be rescued in the same way, and offered fulfillment in a free Homeland.

To understand Weizmann's attachment to his roots, one need only read in his autobiography, the description of his homelife in the "Shtetl":

> We were strangers to the other inhabitants' ways of thought, to each other's dreams, religions, festivals, even languages. There were times when the non-Jewish world was practically excluded from our consciousness, as on the Sabbath, and still more on the spring and autumn festivals. We were separated from the peasants by a whole inner world of memories and experiences. The house was steeped in rich Jewish tradition, and Palestine was at the centre of that ritual. The return was in the air, a vague and deep-rooted Messianism, a hope that would not die.

Weizmann himself left "Shtetl" life when he was enrolled, at the age of eleven, in the secular school in the nearby town of Pinsk. Later, when he showed scientific talent, he moved on to advanced chemical studies in Germany and Switzerland, maintaining himself by giving private tutoring. It was in these student years that he threw himself into Zionism, too busy with chemical research to become an official of the movement, but passionately involved, with a host of student friends, in night-long arguments with communists and many brands of non-Zionist socialists, who had their own solutions for the future. It was a perfect apprenticeship; and as we see from his letters, he not only had a supremely resourceful and intelligent mind, but showed constantly how a new kind of modernity had to be applied to the welfare of the Jewish masses in Eastern Europe. It was these people he thought of constantly; and it was his devotion to them that he communicated to enthusiastic audiences of the same origin at countless meetings throughout the world expounding his Zionist vision.

The return to Zion must be preceded by our return to Judaism.

THEODORE HERZL, 1897

Through a myriad of illustrations in his letters, the devotion comes across most clearly, I think, in a letter he wrote in 1905 to his fiancée Vera in Geneva when he received the news of yet another murderous pogrom in Russia. Weizmann saw it as part of the non-stop sequence of tragedies that had followed the notorious pogrom at Kishinev nearly three years earlier, and which had shaken Jewry to the core. By this time, he had settled in England, and was working on chemical research at the university in Manchester. In his daily letter to Vera, he is frantic:

> God, I am so distraught. I firmly believe that it is a crime and disgrace to be conducting chemical experiments while slaughter takes place over there. The pen is shaking in my hand: my brain refuses to function: everything is tinged with blood. Oh Verochka, it hurts so much. Again and again: and such helplessness. This is my fifth day of suffering the torments of hell. What a pathetic situation to be here, reading the newspapers and teaching Englishmen chemistry!

Such a passionate reaction to a pogrom is understandable. In other letters, as in his major speeches, his eloquence is calm and logical. Yet it was not just the skill of his argument which won over the British political leader Arthur Balfour, when Weizmann was introduced to him in 1906 at an election rally in Manchester, an encounter significant, eleven years later, in the background to the Balfour Declaration favouring the Jewish Homeland in Palestine. Nor was Weizmann's natural eloquence the only factor in securing the support of President Truman, in 1948, for the recognition of the State of Israel. It was the *philosophy* of the man to which they were

121

responding, the conviction he generated that the long history of the Jews had unique and positive meaning for mankind.

One has to reach back to the prophets of the Bible to find the same kind of vision, combining religious faith with convincing political insight. By an extraordinary piece of luck we can see from a letter he wrote at the age of eleven how instinctive this was to him. It was a farewell letter to his old Hebrew teacher, affirming, as he left for his new school at Pinsk, that his Jewish loyalties would never slacken, and to which he then added a remarkable prophecy that only through England would the Jews move to their Homeland:

> Let us carry our banner to Zion, and return to our first mother upon whose knee we were born. For why should we look to the kings of Europe for compassion? In vain! All have decided that the Jews shall die. But England will nevertheless have mercy upon us. To Zion, Jews—to Zion let us go!

Weizmann's schoolboy love of England continued as part of his vision, persisting even in the years in which British government policy in Palestine seemed utterly cruel. This seed of faith seems to have been planted in his mind by the British love of the Bible. This, he believed, had moulded the qualities of liberty and tolerance that he hoped would be equally dominant among his own people, when they experienced freedom.

There is a striking mark of this in a letter he wrote to a friend in New York at the outbreak of the First World War. He had already committed himself to the passion for Zionism that was to dominate his life; but in 1914, Zionist work was centralised in Germany, and Weizmann, who was still pursuing chemical research in Manchester, was horrified at this. He was desperate to wean the Zionist movement from its attachment to that country, and this is how he put it:

> With feverish anxiety I am watching events which have for me a deeper hidden meaning. It is the struggle of the pagan Siegfried against the spirit of the Bible, and the Bible will win.

This antithesis was an astonishingly clear vision of the dreadful events

that would surface in Germany within two decades, and would anni-
hilate a very large part of the Jewish people. No-one can suggest that
Weizmann could have envisaged the scale of the bestiality that would
grip Germany under Hitler; but this unshakable conviction that the
spirituality enshrined in the Bible would ultimately triumph over any
new forms of paganism is a mark of the enduring Bible faith engendered in him by his East European Jewish origins.

The fact that Weizmann himself was based in Manchester turned
out to be of crucial importance to the advancement of his work for
the rebirth of Jewish independence. He had arrived there in 1904,
bringing with him high qualifications in Organic Chemistry based
on years of successful research in Germany, the leader in this field
at the time. His work rapidly expanded and became of national significance in 1914, when research led him into brilliant discoveries that
made it possible to produce acetone, a vital substance in the manu-
facture of munitions and thus a major contribution to Britain's victory in the war. Side-by-side with this, his tireless work for the
creation of a Jewish homeland had attracted the full-hearted support
of C.P. Scott, editor of the great "Manchester Guardian." When
Weizmann's war work on acetone led to his having to move to London to organise large-scale supplies with the Ministry of Munitions,
Scott made it his business to see that Weizmann met the Prime
Minister, Lloyd George, who became attracted by the idea of a
rebirth of the ancestral land. The plan was favoured by most, though
not all, the leading British Jews. The objectors, who included Edwin
Montagu, the India Secretary in Lloyd George's cabinet, felt that a
Homeland for Jews might seem to impugn the citizenship of British Jews. But they were a minority. The Balfour Declaration was
issued on November 2nd, 1917, announcing that the British Government viewed with favour the establishment in Palestine of a
National Home for the Jewish people—a major turning-point in
modern Jewish history.

To the world at large, Weizmann had now become the main Zionist leader, fully at home in the corridors of power, and already legendary among Jews, despite internal rivalries. The style of his Zionist
planning was a natural development from his early emphasis on practical projects in the fields of industry and agriculture. But it was still

*For the Jew,
time predomin-
ates over space
... The world
era is fixed
upon a central
point which
gives meaning
to the process.*

JOSEPH
NEEDHAM

123

There are six million Jews doomed to be pent up in . . . places where they cannot live, and places where they cannot enter.

the *spiritual* vision that expressed his form of Zionist leadership. In essence, his aim was to lead the Jewish masses out of the ghetto to western freedom without sacrificing any of their innate Jewish qualities. This meant, for him, that the renaissance of Jewish life had to flow from within. Many years before the Balfour Declaration, he had launched plans for the foundation of a Hebrew University that would turn the creative work already being done by Jews of the West in science and arts into a product of the Jewish Homeland. A new kind of national pride was to be the key to moral independence. Amid all the problems that surfaced with the eventual birth of Israel, there can be no doubt that this part of the vision has achieved his aim.

The idea of a holy nation meant to the Jews the total absorption of a whole people in the service of an impersonal ideal.

J.L. TALMON

As time went on, there were many battles to be fought within and outside the Zionist movement, with Weizmann's role gradually changing to that of an *éminence* who was already an historical figure. To a great extent, he was no longer in sole practical charge. A major instance was the way he was overshadowed during and after the Second World War by the fighting spirit of the future Prime Minister David Ben Gurion, without which the State would never have emerged. Weizmann, by contrast, was still concentrating on trying to secure a solution by the harnessing of good will. This is not to say that his leadership had lost its personal magic. On great occasions, the mystique around him gave him a voice whose appeal none could match. It is memorable, for instance, that when he appeared in 1937 before the Peel Royal Commission and pleaded for an immediate increase in immigration to Palestine, he spoke even then of "the six million," words seen, after the Holocaust, to have been words of fate. "There are six million Jews," he said, "doomed to be pent up in places where they are not wanted and for whom the world is divided into places where they cannot live, and places where they cannot enter." Ben Gurion said at the time of Weizmann's speech:

> It was perhaps the most penetrating analysis ever given of the plight of the Jewish people, coupled with the strongest and most vigorous claim ever put forward for the immediate creation of the Jewish State.

Weizmann made the same powerful impression when he laid the

Jewish case before the historic Anglo-American Commission of Enquiry in 1946; but primarily it was only as a great figure of the past that he was now acceptable to Israel's new leaders. When the State was founded in 1948, it was inevitable that he should be elected President; but it was equally inevitable, given the political temperature of the time, that he was kept out of any contact with practical policy.

By now he was almost completely blind, and isolated in his own pre-war house some distance from Jerusalem. The parallel that comes to mind instantly is that of Moses, who gave the people of Israel an undying message as he led them from slavery to freedom, but who could take no part in building up the Promised Land. This task, as we read in the final words of the Pentateuch, had to be left to Joshua: Moses was to observe it from afar:

> And Moses went up from the plains of Moab unto the mountains of Nebo, to the top of Pisgah that is over Jericho. And the Lord showed him all the land of Gilead, unto Dan. And all Naphtali, and the land of Ephraim and Menasseh, and all the land of Judah unto the utmost sea. And the Lord said unto him, this is the land which I swore unto Abraham, unto Isaac and unto Jacob, saying I will give it to thy seed. I have caused thee to see it with thine eyes, but thou shalt not go over thither. So Moses the servant of the Lord died there, according to the word of the Lord.

There is no pathos in this end, for Weizmann or for Moses himself. Each had lived a full life, taking the Jewish people far along the road to the future. For Moses, the huge achievement of his life is described imperishably in the Five Books that have come down to us in his name. For Weizmann, the conspectus might seem entirely different; yet at the centre there is also a sense of purpose that draws its strength from a moral drive.

Like Moses, Weizmann was born into a world of slavery that called for redemption. We have followed in this book a story of 2,000 years that began with the destruction of Jerusalem and seemed destined in our own day to face the finality of a second *Churban*. If a miracle has kept the Jewish people alive, it has been fuelled by the sustained memory of the first Exodus. In our own day, Weizmann gave it new meaning.

FOR FURTHER READING

General

Ben-Sasson, H.H. (ed.) *A History of the Jewish People* (Cambridge, 1976)

Finkelstein, Louis (ed.) *The Jews, Their History, Culture and Religion* (New York, 3 vols., 1960)

Kedourie, Elie (ed.) *The Jewish World* (Lavishly Illustrated) (New York, 1979)

Seltzer, Robert M. *Jewish People, Jewish Thought* (New York, 1960)

Individual Subjects

Bernard J. Bamberger: *The Story of Judaism*

Rose Choron: *Family Stories: Travels Beyond the Shtetl*

Lucy Dawidowicz: *The Golden Tradition: Jewish Life in Eastern Europe*

Amos Elon: *Herzl*

Nahum N. Glatzer: *Modern Jewish Thought*

Barry Holtz: *Back to the Sources*

Louis Jacobs: *Principles of the Jewish Faith*

Jacob Katz: *Out of the Ghetto: Social Background of Jewish Emancipation*

Walter Laqueur: *A History of Zionism*

Cecil Roth: *The Jews in the Renaissance*

Howard M. Sachar: *The Course of Modern Jewish History*

Ronald Sanders: *Shores of Refuge: 100 Years of Jewish Emigration*

Norman A. Stillman: *Jews of Arab Lands* (2 vols.)